T0013298

BROKEN LENSES VOLUME 2

Praise for
BROKEN LENSES VOLUME 2

"Emily Bernath has done it again. *Broken Lenses, Volume 2: Seeing Others' Value in a World of Division* is a call to revisit our Bible-based beliefs and to demonstrate them in our daily life. This book brings a refreshing truth of God's perspective and challenges us to unite together in love—seeing ourselves and others the way God sees us. Reading this book will add value to the lives of all who read it."

Jenna Quinn, author of *Pure In Heart* and Jenna's Law,
Founder of Reveal to Heal International

"In *Broken Lenses, Volume 2: Seeing Others' Value in a World of Division*, Emily welcomes her readers into her journey of discovering her value in Christ after sexual assault and how that changed her view towards others. Her workbook-style approach allows thoughtful contemplation and application every step of the way. The reminder of Jesus' ultimate expression of mercy and grace at the cross enabling a relationship with Him possible is the baseline that Emily stands on for how we show respect with love and fairness to other image-bearers.

Worth is determined by God and not our performance. Get to know other people's story. Be who God designed you to be - to abide and be dependent."

Jeff Dalrymple, Executive Director,
Evangelical Council for Abuse Prevention

"Emily is a bright light in our community. From a tumultuous experience with sexual violence, they were able to find freedom within themselves and bring the same warmth and light from within to all of us at UCASA. They're always an inviting and kind presence and we're proud to have them in the community. One of our favorite lines from Emily is "Do not let anyone take away your greatness!"

Utah Coalition Against Sexual Assault, Executive Leadership

"Emily Bernath provides an extraordinary resource for fostering unity in our relationships with one another, as well as a refreshing way to see others. *Broken Lenses, Volume 2: Seeing Others' Value in a World of Division* shows us how to see value in ourselves and in the people around us—the way that God sees our value. This book equips us to be "change-bringers," to speak unity when our world is filled with dividing messages, and offers focus in how we see those around us—and how our views can change for the better."

Angie Fenimore, International Bestselling Author

"Emily Bernath never ceases to amaze and inspire me and her writing does the same. Her faith, quest for truth, and strong convictions come through compassionately and articulately in her writing. Reading Broken Lenses brought me comfort and guidance in my relationship with not only myself but the world around me. I am so grateful to know Emily and for the grace and wisdom she has taught me."

Lauren W, Victim Advocate and Founder of MeToo Many Voices.

"*Broken Lenses, Volume 2: Seeing Others' Value in a World of Division* has been a perfect example of how vulnerability can be strength, courage and empowerment. Reading the book really opened my eyes and brought me closer to Emily. The book has given me a different perspective and I can thank Emily for that!"

Tom Burden, CEO and Founder of Grypmat,
Forbes 30 under 30, Manufacturing & Industry 2019

BROKEN LENSES
VOLUME 2

Seeing Others' Value
in a World of Division

EMILY BERNATH

NASHVILLE

NEW YORK • LONDON • MELBOURNE • VANCOUVER

BROKEN LENSES VOLUME 2
Seeing Others' Value in a World of Division

© 2021 **EMILY BERNATH**

All rights reserved. No portion of this book may be reproduced, stored in a retrieval system, or transmitted in any form or by any means—electronic, mechanical, photocopy, recording, scanning, or other—except for brief quotations in critical reviews or articles, without the prior written permission of the publisher.

Published in New York, New York, by Morgan James Publishing. Morgan James is a trademark of Morgan James, LLC. www.MorganJamesPublishing.com

Unless otherwise noted, scripture is taken from the Good News Bible in Today's English Version—Second Edition, Copyright © 1992 by American Bible Society. Used by permission. All rights reserved.

Scripture quotations marked (NIV) are taken from The Holy Bible, New International Version® (NIV®), Copyright © 1973, 1978, 1984, 2011 by Biblica, Inc.™ Used by permission. All rights reserved worldwide.

Scripture quotations marked (ESV) are from The Holy Bible, English Standard Version, Copyright © 2001 by Crossway Bibles, a publishing ministry of Good News Publishers. Used by permission. All rights reserved.

ISBN 978-1-63195-282-1 paperback
ISBN 978-1-63195-283-8 eBook
Library of Congress Control Number: 2020916118

Cover Design by:
Rachel Lopez
www.r2cdesign.com

Morgan James is a proud partner of Habitat for Humanity Peninsula and Greater Williamsburg. Partners in building since 2006.

Get involved today! Visit
www.MorganJamesBuilds.com

TABLE OF CONTENTS

ACKNOWLEDGMENTS

For someone who never thought they would become an author, I first have to acknowledge that I don't always know what's best for my life. I am grateful for a God who loves me and guides me through this crazy adventure that he has planned for my life, and I wouldn't have it any other way. God never asks us to do something unless it's for our good, and he never calls us to go somewhere unless he has a way planned to make it happen. On my own strength, being an author would have never been my reality, but with God's strength all things are possible. God has also provided me with an amazing community of people to help make this journey possible.

To Alyssa, Carly, Danielle, Kaitlyn, Megan, and Rachel, thank you for taking time out of your weeks to invest in me and for being an amazing group of women to do life together with. Thank you for believing in me and in my message. Even when I wasn't always sure what that message looked like; you all gave me a safe space to figure it out. This book is all about how to see other people as God sees them, and I'm grateful to have people in my life who welcomed me into their journey, provided a place of belonging, and are great friends.

To Angie Fenimore, thank you for continually showing me how to up my abilities as an author and how to keep living out the calling God has laid on my heart with confidence and assurance. To the rest of Calliope Writing Coach crew, thanks for being an awesome tribe. I love getting to be among so many people who are passionate about sharing their messages to the world, and I wish you all the best of luck as you continue to share your unique message. And to my editor, Kathryn, thank you for taking the time to invest and bring life to the message in this book that God has laid on my heart.

To David Hancock and the Morgan James Publishing team, it's an honor to be able to continue working with all of you. Thank you for believing in me and for supporting me every step of the way in the publishing process. You all are the best.

To my parents, thank you for always loving and supporting me in every way you know how. To all of my family, I love you all and wish it was easier to travel across the country to see each other.

To my church family, thank you for continuing to be a source of truth and encouragement in my own life. It's called a walk with God for a reason. It's a journey that never ends, and I'm grateful to have a community of people encouraging me along the way.

Finally, to anyone else who has crossed my path along the way, even if it was only once, thank you. I do not believe in coincidences, and every connection along the way during the course of writing this book happened for a reason.

INTRODUCTION

I love talking to strangers! Whether it's in line at the coffee shop, in an elevator, or at church, I love striking up conversations with new people. Everybody has a story. No two stories are the same, and I enjoy hearing as many different stories as I can.

I say this now, but I wasn't always this way. As a kid, I didn't have much confidence in talking to new people. In fact, I was one of the shyest and quietest kids in my grade throughout my entire childhood.

I gained a tight group of friends at a very young age, and outside that circle of friends I had little social interaction. I always had someone to hang out with, but I didn't place much importance on investing in the lives of the people around me—largely because my lack of investment didn't create many challenges during my childhood.

God made himself real to me for the first time in middle school. I sat in my room almost every night alone and scared. I needed to know someone was there. The first *authentic* prayer I ever made to God was asking him to take away my nightmares, and he did. God answered my prayer on the same night—I didn't have any kind of dream after that night for almost a decade.

I say it was my first authentic prayer because I grew up in church. My family and I went to church almost every week. I knew the Lord's prayer forward and backward, but I didn't make those prayers in church mean anything to me. By not making prayer mean much in my life, its importance didn't carry much depth. I prayed to God only because I needed something. God answered my prayer and life was good. He made himself real to me, but I didn't know God's heart for unity or how he wanted a relationship with me.

God stayed impersonal to me for years, and not much changed about the way I saw God or those around me. When I went to college, I was searching for something new, so I moved to a new city, purposefully separating myself from the place I grew up. I adapted the stereotypical partying lifestyle and quit going to church.

College life was everything I expected it to be—until the night I was raped. Then everything changed. My life? Shattered. My worth? Stripped from me. On that night, I made my second authentic prayer to God, asking him, "Why me, God?" I didn't give God much of a chance to respond. Truthfully, my primary motive was letting him know how mad I was at him.

When I talked with others about what happened to me, I faced questions like, "What did you do?" and "What did you say?" I even got told by someone that it was straight-up my fault. With so much trust broken in such little time, not only with the rapist but with others around me, I didn't know how to see people anymore. I didn't know how they saw me either.

I hated how I felt in my own body. I didn't like looking at myself, and I didn't expect other people to see me any differently. I didn't know how to free myself from the pain I felt, but I knew that what happened to me wasn't my fault. I began to separate myself from a lot of people and soon found myself isolated and lonely. I had hit rock bottom.

In the middle of my darkness, God placed a person in my life who would eternally shift the way I saw others. I didn't know her before being raped, but even after I told her what happened and all I had gone through, she didn't see me as "less than." At a time of my life where my own view of my value was at an all-time low, her view of my value was not conditional to my past. I was valuable enough to her for her to invite me to church, and I gladly accepted her invitation.

By going back to church, I learned how God sees my value. It turns out, I'm valuable enough to God for him to sacrifice the life of his only Son— and I'm not alone. We are all that valuable to God. As I kept attending church, I found people who saw my value in the way God sees my value, and it changed my life forever.

Gaining this new, faith-based, community convicted me to change the way I see value in others. There are way too many people in our world who are where I once was. People everywhere on this earth are hurting, broken, and see their value as "less than." We have the opportunity to be the people in their lives who see them as God sees them—to be people who love them, value them, and recognize their worth.

When we love others and recognize their value, we facilitate an environment of unity. The culture of division our world has and the broken lenses through which our world views people have *no power* over God and his love. I pray that together, we can be people who exhibit God's love to others and bring back the unity God desires and created us for!

—⟋⟍—

As you look at all the destruction going on in this world, have you ever wondered why everyone can't just get along? There are billions of people on this earth. Every one of us was brought here because the God of the universe created us out of love, yet the chaos we see daily speaks anything but love. Out of that same love from which he created us, God sent his Son to earth to die for us. Why? Because we sin.

When we sin, we separate ourselves from God, and God can't stand being separated from us! So, what did God do to mend our separation from him? God stood in our place. He sent Jesus to this earth to live a sinless life, and to take on the death we all deserve as a result of our sin.

> *For the wages of sin is death, but the free gift of God is eternal life in Christ Jesus our Lord. Romans 6:23 ESV*

God is an extremely personal God. His heart is for *unity*. He wants to be united with us and he wants us to be united with one another. If this is what God wants, why don't we see more unity in our world? What is the problem with achieving the kind of unity God desires? Achieving the unity God desires is *not possible* unless we see the same value in those around us that God sees in them!

What do I mean by that? It's simple. When we devalue those around us, we don't treat them as God treats them. Devaluing others makes it that much easier for mistreatment or abuse to occur too—whether the abuse is physical, sexual, verbal, or in any of its other forms. The destruction in this world that comes from abuse results from someone not seeing another as valuable as God sees that person. How, then, do we value those around us as God values them? We *love* them.

If we claim to be disciples of God, loving one another as God loves *isn't* optional. Jesus came to this earth as a perfect demonstration of God's love to others, and he instructs us to do the same.

> *"And now I give you a new commandment: love one another. As I have loved you, so you must love one another. If you have love for one another, then everyone will know that you are my disciples." John 13:34–35*

Jesus makes a bold claim in these verses by saying that if we will just love one another, the world would know we are his disciples, and he's right. Having love for one another means having love for more than just the people we feel like loving. Loving those around us as Jesus loves isn't possible in our own strength and in our human nature, but it *is* possible with God's strength given to us by the Holy Spirit. The Spirit of God, by nature, is a Spirit of unity.

> *Be completely humble and gentle; be patient, bearing with one another in love. Make every effort to keep the unity of the Spirit through the bond of peace. There is one body and one Spirit, just as you were called to one hope when you were called; one Lord, one faith, one baptism; one God and Father of all, who is over all and through all and in all. Ephesians 4:2–6 NIV*

By accepting the payment Jesus gave for our sin as our own, we receive the Holy Spirit and are once again united with God. These verses show us how much God wants oneness and unity. There is only one Holy Spirit, and all who possess it are bound into one body. There is also only one way to receive God's Spirit—by accepting the payment for our sins that Jesus offers us through his death on the cross. Just as we must accept Jesus as our Savior to become one and united with God, we must accept those around us.

> *May the God who gives endurance and encouragement give you the same attitude of mind toward each other that Christ Jesus had, so that with one mind and one voice you may glorify the God and Father of our Lord Jesus Christ. Accept one another, then, just as Christ accepted you, in order to bring praise to God. Romans 15:5–7 NIV*

We can't be people who have the same attitude of mind toward each other as Jesus had unless we love and accept them. Seeing those around us in this way goes against our sinful human nature. In our own nature we do not see others in the way God sees them, but God *gives* us the ability to see others as he sees them.

I pray that we will be people who are willing to see those around us through God's eyes. May we be people who love and accept others, so that we can facilitate an environment with the unity God desires, rather than the division commonly seen in our world. Everyone on this earth has been chosen by God for this time. No one is here by mistake, and everyone has a place of belonging. We are all made in God's image. It is time we start a movement of seeing people in their Godly image rather than their worldly image. God sees everyone on this earth as valuable enough to die for, and I pray this book reveals ways for all of us to see that same value in others and in ourselves.

Chapter One

THEY ARE SEEN

Lesson 1: Sight

Knowing we are seen by someone generates a range of emotions. When we do something good or well, we crave being seen and affirmed in our accomplishments. On the other hand, if we do something wrong or embarrassing, being seen can bring us shame like we've never experienced before.

Emotions aside, being seen creates a greater level of being understood that—deep down—we all want. Seeing people for who they are creates a foundation for us to facilitate the topics that the other chapters in this book will address.

As a child, I was cautious about allowing others to see me deeply. My shy and reserved nature stemmed from a fear of being mistaken— what if they saw me in a way different from how I saw myself? My fear of being misunderstood by others played into my fear of loneliness—if others misunderstood me, they would no longer want to be around me. Night after night, my loneliness controlled me. Most nights, I couldn't fall asleep unless I knew someone was physically there with me. When I finally did fall asleep, I had constant nightmares. Satan was undoubtedly thrilled by seeing me in my room every night terrified of being alone and having nightmares. Satan *loves* it when we feel isolated and hopeless!

When was a time you felt *unseen*? What made you feel that way?

_____

_____

_____

_____

_____

Feeling unnoticed can cause us to think we don't matter—that we have no purpose and nobody cares about us. When those feelings become strong enough, it leads to thoughts of wondering why we're even here on earth and whether we have a place of welcome.

Those things could not be further from the truth—and they are exactly what Satan wants us to believe! One of the strongest lies the enemy feeds to us is that we are unseen and we don't matter. The truth is, no one on this planet is unseen; God sees *everyone*.

The LORD looks down from heaven and sees all of us humans. From where he rules, he looks down on all who live on earth. Psalms 33:13–14

My first experience with God resulted from my fear of loneliness. In my struggle, I was told a simple—yet powerful—message by someone, who said, "We are never alone because God is always with us." I decided to see for myself if that was true. I prayed to God and asked that if he was there to take away my nightmares. The nightmares disappeared, and I slept more peacefully than I had ever slept in my life. Even though I knew nothing about how great God really is, I knew that night that God *saw* me—he was real.

When was a time you felt *seen*? What made you feel that way?

_____

_____

_____

_____

_____

How does it make you feel knowing that God sees you?

_____

_____

_____

_____

See: *verb* to have the power of sight; to have experience of; to perceive the meaning or importance of; to be aware of; to meet with[1]

It's one thing to know God sees us, but what about us seeing him back? I've encountered plenty of people who doubt God exists simply because they can't physically *see* him. But just because we can't see God doesn't

---

1   *Merriam-Webster's Dictionary and Thesaurus,* Updated Edition, s.v. "See."

give evidence for us to conclude that God doesn't exist. We can't see the wind, either, but we know it exists because we can see the effect it has on everything it touches. Slight breezes rustle the leaves in a tree; hurricane velocity winds can knock houses down.

As the definition of *see* indicates, sight is *powerful*. In fact, sight is so powerful, that seeing God's face right now would kill us.

> *Then Moses requested, "Please, let me see the dazzling light of your presence." The LORD answered, "I will make all my splendor pass before you and in your presence I will pronounce my sacred name. I am the LORD, and I show compassion and pity on those I choose. I will not let you see my face, because no one can see me and stay alive,"* Exodus 33:18–20

Like the wind, God also has an effect on everything he touches. We may not be able to see God's face during our time on this earth, but we do get the opportunity to shine God's light to the people in this world. Just as Moses called God's presence a "dazzling light," Jesus speaks of light when appearing to Paul and appointing him to be a light to the world.

> *"But get up and stand on your feet. I have appeared to you to appoint you as my servant. You are to tell others what you have seen of me today and what I will show you in the future. I will rescue you from the people of Israel and from the Gentiles to whom I will send you. You are to open their eyes and turn them from the darkness to the light and from the power of Satan to God, so that through their faith in me they will have their sins forgiven and receive their place among God's chosen people." Acts 26:16–18*

Darkness has no power over light, just as Satan has no power over God. Satan's darkness cannot overcome God's light. As soon as I prayed for God to take away my nightmares, God opened my eyes to his light. From that night on, my fear of loneliness lost its power over me. I knew right then that God saw me; what I didn't know yet was that God calls us to see others in the same way.

God uses us to distribute his light here on earth. If we open our eyes to see those around us, it also opens opportunities to show them God's light. By being a light to others, we get the chance to point them back to God, who has seen them all along.

What do you think it means to have your eyes opened?

_____

_____

_____

_____

How have you seen light overcome darkness in your own life?

_____

_____

_____

_____

What does being a light to others look like for you?

_____

_____

_____

_____

—⚏—

Lesson 2: Perceive

Any time we meet someone new, we begin placing judgment on them within the first few minutes. We then take the little we know about them and begin making assumptions about who they are. This tendency leads many to feel misunderstood—the person they really are isn't the same as the person we perceive them to be.

Our perception of others plays a large role in others feeling like we *see* them, in the way the word is defined: "to perceive the meaning or importance of."[2] My fear of people seeing me was directly linked to their perception of me. I grew up in small town Ohio, where everybody knew everyone. Perceptions were everywhere. It was rare to go anywhere without being seen by a familiar face. I knew how I saw myself, and I didn't want other people to see me in any other way. I tended to just stay quiet and not give people the chance to perceive me wrongly. It felt safer to prevent others from misunderstanding me, but it came at the cost of also preventing them from getting to know me.

When was a time that you felt misunderstood by someone else, and what led you to that experience?

_____

_____

_____

_____

_____

---

2   *Merriam-Webster's Dictionary and Thesaurus,* Updated Edition, s.v. "See."

When have you misunderstood someone else, and what impact did your misunderstanding have on your relationship with that person?

_____

_____

_____

_____

_____

Our misperception of someone can leave them with the experience that we never truly saw them to begin with. What does it look like to perceive someone in a way that makes them feel seen?

Perceive: _verb_ to become aware of through the senses[3]

For the purpose of this lesson, we will stick to becoming more aware through the sense of _sight_. Why is it important for us to make sure those around us know they are seen? Although the concept of making sure we see those around us takes years of life experience, our need to be seen starts on the day we're born. It doesn't take much time for a toddler to approach us and ask us to come see their latest masterpiece, and chances are they won't stop asking us until we go _see_ what they made.

If we aren't fully aware of our surroundings, misperception easily creeps in. When misperception occurs, it creates division rather than the unity God desires.

---

3   _Merriam-Webster's Dictionary and Thesaurus,_ Updated Edition, s.v. "Perceive."

How has your misperception of someone created division in one of your relationships?

_____

_____

_____

_____

_____

What does it look like to become more aware through our senses? In the following passage of Jesus healing a paralyzed man, we see how the people changed their perception of him through their increased awareness:

On one of those days, as he was teaching, Pharisees and teachers of the law were sitting there, who had come from every village of Galilee and Judea and from Jerusalem. And the power of the Lord was with him to heal. And behold, some men were bringing on a bed a man who was paralyzed, and they were seeking to bring him in and lay him before Jesus, but finding no way to bring him in, because of the crowd, they went up on the roof and let him down with his bed through the tiles into the midst before Jesus. And when he saw their faith, he said, "Man, your sins are forgiven you." And the scribes and the Pharisees began to question, saying, "Who is this who speaks blasphemies? Who can forgive sins but God alone?" When Jesus perceived their thoughts, he answered them, "Why do you question in your hearts? Which is easier, to say, 'Your sins are forgiven you,' or to say, 'Rise and walk'? But that you may know that the Son of Man has authority on earth to forgive sins"—he said to the man who was paralyzed—"I say to you, rise, pick up your bed and go home." And immediately he rose up before them and picked up what he had been lying on and went home, glorifying God. And amazement seized them all, and they glorified

God and were filled with awe, saying, "We have seen extraordinary things today." Luke 5:17–26 ESV

When Jesus told the paralyzed man that his sins were forgiven, the initial perception the people had of Jesus was one of blasphemy. I'm guessing the Pharisees thought Jesus was a bit crazy since they replied to Jesus's act of forgiving the man's sins by saying that only God can forgive sins. Jesus followed up the Pharisees' response by perceiving their thoughts and doubt; he then told the paralyzed man to rise and go home. Once the people *saw* this formerly paralyzed man rise up and go home, their perception of Jesus changed immediately from one of blasphemy to one of amazement.

How have you misperceived God and how did that affect your relationship with him?

_____

_____

_____

_____

_____

It's important to note that during his interaction with the paralyzed man, the *character* of Jesus did not change. It was the people's *perception* of Jesus that changed.

The same goes for the way we perceive those around us. Even when they don't change, our perception of them can change. Our first perceptions of people are usually wrong. People are very complex, and trying to perceive someone based on only a few data points about their personality often leads to wrong conclusions.

It's important for us to be willing to let our perceptions of others change. We don't like it when other people perceive us to be someone we're not. In the same way, we shouldn't judge those around us by perceiving them to be someone they aren't.

On the night when I asked God to take away my nightmares, I received a perception of God I had never seen before. God made himself real to me in a tangible way. Along with knowing I was seen by him, I was able to see him as real instead of as some being created through imagination.

Having this moment with God was powerful, but it didn't change the way I perceived the people around me. What it did do was give me context into the power that being seen in a different light can have.

How has your perception of someone else changed over time, and what allowed you to see them differently?

_____

_____

_____

_____

_____

—〰—

Lesson 3: Meeting

Two of the most dreadful words for a student to hear during class are *group project*. In the more than twenty years I spent in school, I can't recall a single time where one of my classes experienced pure joy from getting assigned a group project. But why?

Group projects require teamwork and meeting with other people to get the project done. Organizing the meeting means finding a time to fit that busy person's schedule, and even after it's scheduled, it involves trying to track down the person who never responds. This stigma is no different in the corporate world. Many professionals see meetings as a big waste of time because they prevent them from performing their regular duties.

Unlike the reputation meetings have earned in the corporate world, God sees meeting with others as something of utmost importance. In fact, God commands us to not give up on meeting together.

Let us hold on firmly to the hope we profess, because we can trust God to keep his promise. Let us be concerned for one another, to help one another to show love and to do good. Let us not give up the habit of meeting together, as some are doing. Instead, let us encourage one another all the more, since you see that the Day of the Lord is coming nearer. Hebrews 10:23–25

Do you find importance in meeting with others? Why or why not?

_____

_____

_____

_____

What reasons have you had in the past for avoiding meeting with people?

_____

_____

_____

_____

Where the world and God begin to differ on the topic of meeting with others is in the *intention* of the meeting itself. The world focuses more on the result or the productivity that comes from the meeting, and less about the well-being of the people in the meeting.

The verses in Hebrews indicate that our meetings with others should instead focus on encouraging one another to live a life full of love and good deeds. How would our meetings here on earth look different if we had them with the intention of spurring one another on toward love and good deeds? My guess is that those meetings would not resemble the meetings we have now.

How has someone else encouraged you to live a life of love and good deeds? What impact did they have on you?

_____

_____

_____

_____

_____

In Paul's first letter to the Thessalonians, he goes more in depth on the matter of encouraging one another toward love and good deeds.

Now we ask you, brothers and sisters, to acknowledge those who work hard among you, who care for you in the Lord and who admonish you. Hold them in the highest regard in love because of their work. Live in peace with each other. And we urge you, brothers and sisters, warn those who are idle and disruptive, encourage the disheartened, help the weak, be patient with everyone. Make sure that nobody pays back wrong for wrong, but always strive to do what is good for each other and for everyone else. Rejoice always, pray continually, give thanks in all circumstances; for this is God's will for you in Christ Jesus. 1 Thessalonians 5:12–18 NIV

If we lived in a world where we all truly encouraged the disheartened, helped the weak, and strove to do good for everyone, how many people in this world would feel unseen? *Zero.*

Every single person on this planet has felt the effects of being disheartened or weak in some area. We are called to be people who help and encourage others in those times.

The tendencies to show patience, encourage the disheartened, and help the weak, do not readily exist within our human nature. However, they *are* all possible when we have God's strength and guidance in our lives. With his strength, we have the ability to create an environment full of people who feel encouraged, loved, and, in turn, seen.

Which of the following is *easiest* for you to do: encouraging the disheartened, helping the weak, being patient, or always striving to do good for others. Why is it easiest for you?

_____

_____

_____

_____

Of the characteristics mentioned in the question above, which is the *hardest* for you to do and why?

_____

_____

_____

_____

—m—

Lesson 4: Experience

Imagine this, you're getting coffee, catching up with a good friend, and your friend tells you that they've broken a world record. Unless your friend is particularly well-known for being exceptional at something, you likely don't believe them. You may even go so far as to say to them, "I'll have to *see* it to believe it." In alignment to the definition, "to have experience of,"[4] you want to have the *experience* of watching them accomplish this feat before you believe them.

What is something you had to experience, or see, to believe?

_____

_____

_____

_____

_____

_____

Our life on earth is built upon experiences. Each of us has a combination of experiences unique to any other person in the world. Our experiences play a huge role in determining how we see the world. When we encounter a bad experience with a person or group, it can create a negative association to our future interactions with that same person or group—we don't see them in the same way. We all have our fair share of bad experiences—the suffering in this world is real.

Although it is true that God doesn't enjoy watching our struggles, pain and suffering aren't going away from earth—unless every person in

---

4   *Merriam-Webster's Dictionary and Thesaurus,* Updated Edition, s.v. "See."

this world commits to never sinning again, and I don't see that happening any time soon. While none of us particularly enjoy going through bad experiences, it is often in our times of suffering that we grow the most.

Sometimes it takes a painful experience to make us change our ways.
Proverbs 20:30

God used my fear of loneliness—and the pain that came from it—to initially draw me into his presence. His work in that area of my life didn't stop there though. Knowing the depth of the pain I felt in my fear of isolation, and the peace I felt after asking God to take my fear away, changed the way I saw God. Instead of seeing God as just some arbitrary entity in the sky, God became someone who, at the very least, I knew could hear me.

As I moved from middle school into high school, I became more open to being seen by and socializing with people outside my core group of friends. The people around me didn't change—I had gone to school with the same 150 people since kindergarten. What changed was my ability to recognize more people around me because I spent a lot less time concerned about having to supply an answer to my own loneliness.

How has a painful experience of yours changed your ways?

_____

_____

_____

_____

_____

When we involve God in the changing of our ways, that change will *always* be good.

We know that in all things God works for good with those who love him, those whom he has called according to his purpose. Romans 8:28

God is not blind to the brokenness of this world. God sees each of us and uses the pain we go through for the good of those around us. If we move away from believing that the world is against us, and toward believing that God always makes something good from our story, we become free to see those around us differently.

How has God allowed you to see someone differently than you once did?

_____

_____

_____

_____

_____

As Paul describes in his letter to the Galatians, freedom is a calling we have, and we are to use that freedom to love those around us.

As for you, my friends, you were called to be free. But do not let this freedom become an excuse for letting your physical desires control you. Instead, let love make you serve one another. For the whole Law is summed up in one commandment: "Love your neighbor as you love yourself." Galatians 5:13–14

After stating our calling for freedom, notice that Paul first distinguishes what we *shouldn't* use our freedom for. God is not giving us permission to act as we please, but rather to love those around us. Truly loving someone without first seeing them *isn't possible*. And I'm not talking about physically seeing them—someone's looks should have no influence over our decision to love them. Seeing someone simply means we recognize the fact that they are a creation of God and that they hold just as much value as everyone else on this earth.

How have you let your physical desires prevent you from loving those around you?

_____

_____

_____

_____

_____

How can you serve those around you out of love?

_____

_____

_____

_____

_____

Dear God,

You saw me in my mother's womb and you see everyone on this earth. Knowing that you see me gives me the power to combat Satan in any instance where he tries to tell me I don't matter. Satan has no power over your light, and you call me to be your light to those around me. I confess that I often misperceive others, and when I do, it leaves them with the experience of being unseen. You see everyone through a lens of love, and you are capable of miracles that seem blasphemous to the human eye. You call me to be intentional in meeting with others, and I pray for you to give me an opportunity to meet with someone who needs to know that they are seen first and foremost by you. I desire to be the kind of person who leaves others with the experience that they matter. Thank you for being a God who uses all of our experiences for good and I pray that I will be able to see all of the experiences you lead me through with that mindset.

In Jesus' name,

Amen.

Chapter Two

THEY ARE EQUAL

Lesson 1: Same

Finding what x equals remains the greatest mystery for any algebra student. If someone gave us an equation and asked us to find the value for x, how would we solve for it? The short answer is to do whatever it takes to get x by itself on one side of the equation. But why? In math, an equal sign means that the value on each side of the equation is the same. If we find x by itself on one side of the equal sign, it by association equals the number remaining on the other side. Okay, enough math for one day. (As a math tutor for the past decade, I get carried away easily.)

How can we apply this same concept of being *equal* to the way we see those around us? One of the ways to see those around us as equal is to see them all in the same light.

Equal: *adjective* of the same measure, quantity, value, quality, number, degree, or status as another; regarding or affecting all objects in the same way: impartial[5]

When I say we should view everyone in the same light, I recognize that each of us has been made uniquely by God and has a unique purpose. My main objective in that statement is exploring this thought: how different would our world look if we treated everyone around us as if we saw the same value in each of them?

I'm sure a lot of us would like to think we see the same value in everyone. The truth is, none of us sees the same value in everyone. Biases in this world are real. We all have them, and we are all affected by them.

There is no environment quite like high school when it comes to demonstrating the way bias impacts the way we interact with and see those around us. The constant peer pressure to maintain a certain image and perform at a certain level creates the perfect arena for the enemy to step in and play the game of telling us we aren't as valuable as our other classmates.

When I started high school, my approach to seeing those around me shifted. I branched out some and began to be more comfortable communicating with the people around me. I made many amazing friends in high school that I'm still in touch with. However, the motivation for my communication was driven more by me seeing equal value in our interests than by purely seeing their value as another human being.

My issue was how often I prevented valuable connections and friendships because I allowed biases to tell me it wasn't worth it. Those biases included things like, they're part of this friend group and I'm not, or they like this subject and I don't. Because everyone knows that the theater kids and the sports players can't be friends, right? Obviously, the answer to that question is *no*. Yet so many of us are guilty of operating in that mindset, often subconsciously.

---

5   *Merriam-Webster's Dictionary and Thesaurus,* Updated Edition, s.v. "Equal."

What is a bias you possess, and how does it impact the value you see in those around you?

_____

_____

_____

_____

_____

How have you been impacted by the biases of someone else and the value they saw in you?

_____

_____

_____

_____

The people in the Bible were no different from us today. They carried biases of their own and they also saw varying degrees of value in others. Here we see a perfect example of a bias coming to play through people showing favoritism:

My brothers and sisters, believers in our glorious Lord Jesus Christ must not show favoritism. Suppose a man comes into your meeting wearing a gold ring and fine clothes, and a poor man in filthy old clothes also comes in. If you show special attention to the man wearing fine clothes and say, "Here's a good seat for you," but say to the poor man, "You stand there" or "Sit on the floor by my feet," have you not discriminated among yourselves and become judges with evil thoughts? James 2:1–4 NIV

As James points out, "believers in our glorious Lord Jesus Christ must not show favoritism." It's important to note that James isn't giving unbelievers permission to show favoritism as they please. Instead, he is holding believers to a higher level of accountability.

Essentially, James is saying that if we are a believer of the Lord Jesus Christ, showing favoritism is *unacceptable*! Why is that such an important distinction? If we want to avoid showing favoritism, we need to view everyone as having equal value.

But James doesn't stop his bold declarations there. Later in that passage James calls us out by saying we are "judges with evil thoughts." Initially, I thought that was a little harsh. I mean, how dare he? But the truth is, James is right. God does not judge people in the same ways we do.

For God judges everyone by the same standard. Romans 2:11

God judges us all the same, or *equally*. Any of our thoughts that result in discrimination or valuing people by different sets of standards, are not thoughts from God! God and all of his ways are good. While the world judges in a way that discriminates, God judges in a way that brings freedom.

Speak and act as people who will be judged by the law that sets us free. James 2:12

The law that sets us free is found in Jesus. The standard God sets is that when we sin, the payment we owe is death. When we receive Jesus's payment for our sin, God judges our payment in Jesus's death, which frees us from having to die as well. God makes this same judgment for everyone. There's no one on this planet that Jesus's sacrifice can't cover—all we need to do is receive his sacrifice.

How have you experienced freedom by being judged by God's standards rather than the world's standards?

_____

_____

_____

_____

_____

What does it mean to speak and act as a person who is judged by the law that sets you free?

_____

_____

_____

_____

_____

What is a step you can take in your life toward judging everyone by the same standard?

_____

_____

_____

_____

_____

Lesson 2: Impartial

Suppose it's a Friday night, and you're making plans with a friend to go out for dinner. Your friend gives you a couple of options to choose from, both of which you enjoy *equally*. Which one do you pick? If both options have equal value to you, then you are *impartial*[6] to the decision made. In other words, it doesn't matter which restaurant you go to, you'll get the same satisfaction from each.

Our human nature works in a way that when there's a decision to be made, we pick the option that will bring us the most value in return. When we make decisions based solely on their return value, we create a society of people who neglect the needs of those around us. We care only about what's good for us.

To see those around us equally, we need to not only see them as having equal value with respect to one another, but also as having an equal value with respect to *us*.

How does showing partiality to the people around us change the way we interact with them? What about the opposite? Truly not showing partiality to others requires us to see the same level of value in them as we see in ourselves.

When was the last time you made a decision in which you *did* show partiality and what was the result?

_____

_____

_____

_____

_____

6   *Merriam-Webster's Dictionary and Thesaurus,* Updated Edition, s.v. "Equal."

When was the last time you made a decision in which you *did not* show partiality, and what was the result?

_____

_____

_____

_____

_____

High school culture is a breeding ground for partiality. Influences like dating go into effect and suddenly the reasons we used to hang out and see people are no longer valid. That wasn't the case with me, though. My high-school self acted a lot more like my younger self when it came to boys and dating—I stayed silent. For a good portion of high school, I refused to talk with my friends about any interest I had in guys largely because I hated the assumptions I thought would be made as a result.

Instead, my partiality came out in different ways. Most of the people I went to high school with perceived me as one of the "smart ones," and I tended to be partial to others in my class who were also perceived in that way. I played a lot of sports too, but not the "cool" sports. That allowed me to be friends with a lot of other athletes without earning the title of a "jock," because I was also partial to not having labels put on me.

There's nothing wrong with making friends and finding interest in people who share hobbies and fields of study—we all do it. Where partiality becomes a problem is taking those same reasons and using them as the basis by which we see value in others. When we see any person in that mindset, it creates division, and that couldn't make the enemy any happier! For us to be people who see others the way God sees them, we cannot show partiality.

So Peter opened his mouth and said: "Truly I understand that God shows no partiality, but in every nation anyone who fears him and does what is right is acceptable to him." Acts 10:34–35 ESV

Have you had a moment when you knew that you were truly accepted by God? If so, what was it? If not, how can you ask God to show his acceptance to you?

_____

_____

_____

In his statement, Peter brings to light the subject of fear by declaring that we are to fear God—but why? When it comes to this world, *fear* often stems from a sense of insecurity. If we're insecure about our body image, it creates a fear of being seen. If we're insecure about our talents, it generates a fear of displaying them.

Insecurities also come in areas that others see as our strengths, not just weaknesses. People perceiving me as smart also made me not want to be perceived as stupid. Not wanting to be perceived as stupid created within me a fear of being wrong. The effect of that fear? I didn't give myself permission to fail and grow. I stuck to the areas I knew I was good at. In my mind, failing and being wrong would have lessened my value and given others permission to see me as less equal as they did before.

What is an insecurity you have dealt with, and what fear have you experienced as a result of that insecurity?

_____

_____

_____

Anything that causes us to have fear in the things of this world is not from God! God both wants to deliver and is fully capable of delivering us from every single one of our worldly fears.

I sought the LORD, and he answered me; he delivered me from all my fears. Psalms 34:4 NIV

Has God delivered you from a past fear? What was the fear and how were you delivered from it?

_____

_____

_____

If God is capable of delivering us from all our earthly fears, what does it look like to instead place our fear in him? Unlike placing fear in the things of this world, fear placed in God comes with many benefits:

Life: *The fear of the LORD is a fountain of life, that one may turn away from the snares of death. Proverbs 14:27 ESV*
Confidence: *In the fear of the LORD one has strong confidence, and his children will have a refuge. Proverbs 14:26 ESV*
Blessings: *Blessed is everyone who fears the LORD, who walks in his ways! Psalms 128:1 ESV*

When we place our fear in the things of this world, we experience shame, timidity, and condemnation, instead of the life, confidence, and blessings God has for us. Fear in this world has no power over God. The life, confidence, and blessings that come from placing our fear in God are an equal opportunity open to all who are willing to trust that God will provide for them.

How have you experienced the life, confidence, or blessings as described in the verses above?

_____

_____

_____

_____

Lesson 3: Just

Tune into the evening news, and it won't take long before you hear a story involving a cry for justice. A large part of those cries for justice are born from the desire for equal treatment. The number of avenues for any one of us to speak up and have our voices heard are greater than ever before. The increase in ease of getting our voices heard about the injustice of this world forces us to address justice to a greater degree.

Where do you see a lack of justice in your life and how does that lack of justice make you feel unequal to those around you?

_____

_____

_____

_____

Just: *adjective* guided by truth, reason, justice, and fairness[7]

---

[7] *Dictionary.com,* s.v. "Just," accessed June 27, 2020, https://www.dictionary.com/

The quality of being *just* is a synonym to *equal*.[8] Similar to the concept of fairness, we all have the desire for justice. When we see bad things happen in the world, we want something to be done about it, but we don't always go about executing those actions well. Even though the demand for justice in this world often gets executed in unhealthy ways, the desire for justice itself can be extremely healthy. God himself shares the same desire for justice, and it is in God's nature to be just. God *loves* justice.

The LORD says, "I love justice and I hate oppression and crime. I will faithfully reward my people And make an eternal covenant with them. Isaiah 61:8

What do you think it means to love justice?

_____

_____

_____

_____

What does the fact that God loves justice say about his character?

_____

_____

_____

_____

Even though both God and our world love justice, they execute their love for justice in completely opposite ways. Justice in this world is largely absent of grace and mercy, and groups of people all over the world become

---

8   *Merriam-Webster's Dictionary and Thesaurus,* Updated Edition, s.v. "Equal."

oppressed in the name of "justice." I'm not saying that having a justice system isn't important, because it is, but the way our world administers justice doesn't always come from a healthy place. Contrary to our world's view of justice, God's view of justice looks like this:

> And the word of the LORD came again to Zechariah: "This is what the LORD Almighty said: 'Administer true justice; show mercy and compassion to one another. Do not oppress the widow or the fatherless, the foreigner or the poor. Do not plot evil against each other.'" Zechariah 7:8–10 NIV

In addition to God's love for justice is his love for us. Justice plays a core role in God's plan for making that eternal covenant with us. What does that covenant look like? We see from the verse in Isaiah that God's justice *doesn't* involve oppression and crime. In other words, any attempts to bring justice that involve either oppression or crime are *not from God!* In order to show true justice, we need to show mercy and compassion to those around us. What does showing justice in this way look like?

> Get rid of all bitterness, rage and anger, brawling and slander, along with every form of malice. Be kind and compassionate to one another, forgiving each other, just as in Christ God forgave you. Ephesians 4:31–32 NIV
>
> Therefore, as God's chosen people, holy and dearly loved, clothe yourselves with compassion, kindness, humility, gentleness and patience. Bear with each other and forgive one another if any of you has a grievance against someone. Forgive as the Lord forgave you. Colossians 3:12–13 NIV

We can't be people with mercy and compassion for those around us unless we are willing to forgive. Chances are, if we don't see them as having equal value to ourselves and everyone else, the odds of us showing mercy or compassion to others aren't very high.

When we seek mercy from others, we've likely done something we shouldn't have, and we want to be forgiven and freed from it. Nobody loves showing mercy as much as God does, and it is out of mercy for us that God gave us his Son to transform us from death to life.

> But because of his great love for us, God, who is rich in mercy, made us alive with Christ even when we were dead in transgressions—it is by grace you have been saved. Ephesians 2:4–5 NIV

During high school, I was at a place in life where I knew God was real. I prayed to receive him into my life, but I hadn't yet truly been transformed by his grace. My high school self knew little about what it looked like to show mercy. I did the best I knew how at being nice to all who were around me, but I wasn't good at speaking with compassion to others. Speaking with the absence of compassion, even when done with good intention, can give others the impression that we don't care about them.

Thankfully, God is a lot more merciful in nature than we are. When God had mercy on us—when he sacrificed his Son to make all of us who are dead to our sin come alive again—he did so as an act of true justice. God knows the payment for our sin is death. He also knows we can't make that payment on our own accord, so he sent Jesus to die in our place. By accepting Jesus's payment as our own, our sins have already been paid for! We become alive, rather than staying dead to our sin—talk about good news!

How has God shown mercy or compassion to you personally?

_____

_____

_____

How can you have mercy or compassion for someone else?

_____

_____

_____

—m—

Lesson 4: Fair

The desire for equality begins at a very young age. It doesn't matter what is involved, if a parent gave an older child permission to do something that a younger child wasn't allowed to do, what would the younger sibling's response be? That's right, the younger child would say, "That's not *fair!*"[9] As the youngest of six siblings, one could say I'm pretty familiar with this situation.

What the younger sibling really communicates when they say "That's not fair!" is the fact that they want to be treated *equally* to the older sibling. Encountering unfair circumstances in life doesn't go away in adulthood, it just shows itself in different ways. Unfairness looks like putting in massive effort toward earning a promotion, only to watch someone else get the promotion instead. Unfairness also looks like losing a loved one much sooner than expected and not getting the time we wanted with them.

When was a time you were treated *unfairly*, and how did it make you feel?

_____

_____

_____

_____

---

9   *Merriam-Webster's Dictionary and Thesaurus,* Updated Edition, s.v. "Equal."

When was a time that you were treated *fairly*, and how did it make you feel?

_____

_____

_____

_____

Which of those questions was easier to answer? I'm going to bet it was the one about being treated unfairly. We all have preconceived notions about what fairness is, and we often have no problem whatsoever expressing when they aren't met.

As high school progressed, I experienced my first real loss of a friendship. I couldn't say what happened other than because we entered a new season in life, our interests changed. The change in interests led to a decision that we weren't friends like we used to be. What I can say, is that high-school me thought I had been treated unfairly.

I am a person who highly values friendships and I do as much as I can to be there for others, so what happened came as a surprise to me. And I wasn't the only person it came as a surprise to either—had the topic been brought up with other friends of mine at the time, they would have validated my feelings of being treated unfairly.

What does fairness really look like though? To no surprise, the Bible puts a different spin on fairness.

I am not trying to relieve others by putting a burden on you; but since you have plenty at this time, it is only fair that you should help those who are in need. Then, when you are in need and they have plenty, they will help you. In this way both are treated equally. 2 Corinthians 8:13–14

Contrary to the world's consumer-driven culture, the fairness displayed in these verses happens in the spirit of giving. Paul specifically states that giving isn't intended to be a burden, but rather an exchange done out of fairness. In order to give in this way, we must give up our selfishness and believe that those we give to deserve what we have just as much as we do.

Even though I may have been "right" in my feelings of unfairness over the loss of my friend, my perception of fairness didn't facilitate an environment in which I could get what I actually wanted—a restored friendship. A main factor in preventing that from happening was the way in which I viewed fairness. By viewing fairness from what I felt like I should be *receiving*, rather than how I could have helped *provide* a need, I didn't set myself up for cultivating the restoration I desired.

There are a few different things I like about the passage in Second Corinthians. First, Paul starts by declaring how the mission isn't to burden one person in order to relieve another. The heart of his declaration is one of equality.

He then states how the fair thing to do when we have plenty is to give to those in need. Essentially, Paul says, "How *unequal* do we have to see those around us that we *wouldn't* give to someone in need if we have plenty to offer?" Talk about a reality check! The truth is, none of us is any better than the person next to us, and we all deserve to have our needs met.

What is something you have a plentiful supply of, and how could you give part of your plenty to someone in need?

_____

_____

_____

_____

Paul finishes the passage by indicating that we might not always be the one in the position of having plenty. Therefore, when we have the ability, we should give as we would want someone else to give to us if we were the one in need. Then if we become the one in need, it's important to remember that our need does not diminish our value as a person.

We don't have to feel unequal to others because we have a need that they don't—we all have needs. Operating in the mindset of being a person who uses what we have plenty of to supply the needs of others creates a culture that brings unity. God loves us all equally. He saw our need to be freed from the bondage of our sin. He had plenty of grace to offer to us in our bondage, and out of that grace he gave his Son's life for ours to restore our unity with him. In the world's definition of *fairness*, it isn't fair that Jesus died a death he didn't deserve. One could also say it's not fair for us to reap the benefit of an eternal life we didn't *personally* earn. Luckily for us, God's definition of fairness looks like helping those in need. We are the ones who are in need, and Jesus helped us by dying on the cross in our place in exchange for eternal life with God.

How has someone else given to you when you were in a time of need and what effect did it have on you?

_____

_____

_____

_____

_____

Dear God,

Help me to be more aware of my biases and how they hinder me from seeing everyone around me equally. You are a God who judges everyone by the same standard. Thank you for giving me the option to take your Son's payment for my sins as my own so that I can be judged in a law that gives freedom. You are not a God who shows partiality, and you see the same value in me as you do everyone on this earth. I come to you now and ask for deliverance from my worldly fears. I pray against anything the enemy keeps throwing my way to bring up those fears so I may live my life more confidently in you. You love justice and you bless all who walk in your ways. Provide me with your mercy and compassion for others so I can be a person who shows true justice, just as you did for me when Jesus died on the cross. Thank you for being a plentiful giver, and show me how I can give what I have plenty of to someone in need.

In Jesus' name,

Amen.

Chapter Three

THEY ARE BRANCHES

Lesson 1: Division

The nature of this chapter is the easiest to visualize in imagery—anyone who has ever seen a tree or watched a Bob Ross painting show knows what a branch looks like. This chapter is also likely the hardest to visualize in the context of seeing others as God sees them. To be clear, I'm not saying we should visualize those around us as trees. However, in part of Jesus's teaching, he brings up an analogy using branches:

"I am the vine, and you are the branches. Those who remain in me, and I in them, will bear much fruit; for you can do nothing without me." John 15:5

Branches play a very specific role on a tree. They bear fruit, and the quality of the fruit depends on the life that the branch receives from the rest of the tree. In these verses, Jesus uses the analogy of bearing fruit to make a bold comparison. He says that if we remain in him, we will bear much fruit, and if we don't remain in him, we can do nothing. The fruit that Jesus speaks of in this passage is spiritual fruit, but the comparison remains true for any physical branch as well—when a branch falls off an apple tree, the branch no longer produces apples.

What does "remaining in Jesus" mean to you?

_____

_____

_____

_____

_____

_____

For the purpose of this chapter, I want to set aside any judgment about the quantity of fruit those around us produce. I want to instead focus on the roles of the branches.

> **Branch:** *noun* a division (as of an antler or a river) related to a whole like a plant branch to its stem; a discrete element of a complex system: as a) a separate but dependent part of a central organization b) a division of a family descended from one ancestor[10]

The first attribute of branches we see from that definition is that of *division.* Most of us relate to the word *division* in a negative context. Some have a bad association with the word *division* because it can indicate disagreement between different groups. Others have a bad association with

---

10   *Merriam-Webster's Dictionary and Thesaurus,* Updated Edition, s.v. "Branch."

the word from bad experiences in math class. (I personally can't relate to that because I did math for fun as a kid, but I know plenty of others who can relate.)

One way to look at division is through the lens of separation, such as dividing up portions of a meal. Division in this way is not the same as the division that takes place among branches. There is a huge difference between having divisions and being divided!

As I graduated high school and went to college, I purposefully branched off from everyone I grew up with. I went to a college away from home that no one else from my graduating class attended. I didn't make this move in an act to divide or separate myself from my high-school friends—in fact, I regularly came back home to hang out with them. What I *did* want to do was branch off and form new friendships in this new phase of life.

Similarly, when Jesus speaks in John 15, he speaks from an angle of *unity*, not separation!

"Remain united to me, and I will remain united to you. A branch cannot bear fruit by itself; it can do so only if it remains in the vine. In the same way you cannot bear fruit unless you remain in me." John 15:4

Describe a time you *didn't* involve Jesus in a situation; what was the result?

_____

_____

_____

_____

_____

Describe a time you *did* involve Jesus in a situation; what was the result?

_____

_____

_____

_____

Did you notice any differences in the results of those two situations? If so, what?

_____

_____

_____

_____

When we, the branches, remain in Jesus, the vine, we bear fruit to the benefit of more than just ourselves. Just as the apples produced from the branch of an apple tree can be eaten by anyone who crosses the tree's path, there is no limit to how much God will use the fruit we bear to bless those he puts on our path.

Branching off into a new community in college presented me with an ample number of opportunities to bear new fruit to those around me. The problem was that I had no interest in involving Jesus in any of those situations, and the relational fruit I produced as a result suffered.

Instead of turning to Jesus, I turned to alcohol and talking to guys at parties. As a result, most of the relationships I formed with those around me were as superficial as the "joy" I experienced every time I got drunk. Of course, I can say that with confidence only now that I'm on the other side of it all. Back then, I believed I was doing the whole college thing the way everyone else did.

How has the fruit you've produced been a blessing to those around you?

_____

_____

_____

_____

_____

How have you been blessed by the fruit produced by someone else?

_____

_____

_____

_____

_____

—⧑—

Lesson 2: Discrete

Everyone living on this earth contains a few basic needs for survival; one of those needs is water. Like all physical matter, water is made up of a combination of elements—the chemical formula for water is H_2O.

Though simple, the elements that make up water carry extreme significance. If we compare water with hydrogen peroxide, H_2O_2, we see that the formulas are just one oxygen off, but how these two compounds interact with their environments are completely different. While we need to consume water to live, if we consumed hydrogen peroxide in the same way, it would be extremely hazardous to our bodies.

We see the word *elements* used in the definition of "branch," "a discrete element in a complex system."[11]

Discrete: *adjective* individually distinct[12]

In water's case, those elements are two hydrogen atoms and one oxygen atom. In the case of the branches from the vine that is Jesus, those elements are us. No one else will ever be the exact same branch as us, because God made each of us individually and unique. Contrary to the jealousy-filled world in which we live—a world that constantly tells us we should be more like everyone else—it is of utmost importance that we live as the unique individual God created us to be. Think about it, if water decided it wanted to be more like hydrogen peroxide instead, we would all be left without one of life's necessities.

Every time I went out and got drunk, I fell victim to the "being more like everyone else" mentality. Was I keeping up with the drink counts of everyone else? Will that cute guy over there notice me?

All of this was new territory for me. I never drank in high school—I had no reason to. Between playing sports in every season, doing all the homework, and hanging out with friends, I didn't have time for anything else. But college was a whole different story. College is that time of life to party your life away, right? Figuratively speaking, that's exactly what I did.

A large part of why I drank was because inside, I had no sense of my identity. I did not see myself as "individually separate or distinct"

11   *Merriam-Webster's Dictionary and Thesaurus,* Updated Edition, s.v. "Branch."
12   *Merriam-Webster's Dictionary and Thesaurus,* Updated Edition, s.v. "Discrete."

from everyone else. Instead, I did the opposite and blended in with the cultural norm.

People don't get drunk at parties expecting to form deep and meaningful relationships with the others at the party; getting drunk is more about "having a good time" and "making memories." Let's be honest—it's an accomplishment just to remember what happened the night before when waking up from a long night out. Forget being present enough when talking to someone at a party for them to know they are seen and heard by us.

In what areas has the world told you to be more like someone else?

_____

_____

_____

_____

_____

What does God say about you in those same areas?

_____

_____

_____

_____

_____

Although I was great at taking the world's advice when it came to partying, I didn't always agree with the world's view on relationships. I didn't enter college with the expectation of finding a future husband, and I had no interest in having sex with anyone. Sure, it left some men disappointed, but I knew that wasn't what I wanted, and I stuck to it.

It's not always easy for us to mute the voice of the world surrounding us, a voice that always tells us what we should be. But the more we know our unique value, the easier it becomes.

> *Everything that God has created is good; nothing is to be rejected, but everything is to be received with a prayer of thanks, because the word of God and the prayer make it acceptable to God. 1 Timothy 4:4–5*

God created us, and everything God creates is good. What this means for us is that everything given to us by God, that makes us the unique individual we are, is good. Anything telling us that the person God made us to be *isn't* good is a lie!

Do you see any attributes of the person God made you to be as not being good?

_____

_____

_____

_____

_____

What is the truth behind those attributes?

_____

_____

_____

_____

_____

Even though nothing in my life leading up to college caused me to own the identity of a "bad" person, deep down, I craved more. I didn't want people to just see me as a "good" person just because I didn't do bad things. I wanted to be seen as "good" in a more personal way. I wanted to be seen as *Emily*. The problem? I didn't even know who *Emily* was. I didn't know how to see myself for my unique value, and I didn't know how to see those around me for their unique value either.

Because of my blindness to the individual God made me to be, I fell captive to the comparison and judgment of the world. Drinking allowed me to feel relevant in my new phase of life. At the same time, drinking clouded my brain enough to destroy any potential capacity to figure out who I was. Getting drunk also took away my ability to be a light to those around me. Besides, even if I tried to be a bright light to those around me while in my foggy state of mind, it wouldn't have worked. Bright lights in fog make the vision of our surroundings worse than it was before.

While my uncertainty of my true identity didn't cause division between me and those around me, it also didn't create an environment for connecting well with others. If we don't know which part of the body we are, then we don't know which part of the body we were meant to be connected to in order to bring the unity God desires.

When we are able to see the individual God made us to be as good, comparison and judgment from the world loses its effect on us. Living in who God made us to be allows us to also be a light to those around us.

"You are the light of the world. A city set on a hill cannot be hidden. Nor do people light a lamp and put it under a basket, but on a stand, and it gives light to all in the house. In the same way, let your light shine before others, so that they may see your good works and give glory to your Father who is in heaven." Matthew 5:14–16 ESV

How are you shining your light to those around you?

_____

_____

_____

—〰—

Lesson 3: Dependent

It's a new morning, the alarm on your phone has just gone off, and you look at its screen to see the date of April 15th. The end of every adult's favorite season has arrived—tax season. When it comes to doing taxes, an important detail is the declaration of *dependents*, or people who are dependent on a source of income. Every child remains a dependent of their parents' income throughout childhood, but income is just one example of showing dependence.

Every baby immediately enters a world of complete dependence at birth. Babies cannot feed, transport, clean, or speak for themselves. As our life evolves, we learn and gain independence.

As humans, we *love* independence. The more independent we become, the harder it is for us to admit when we are dependent on something. It's human nature for us to want to prove that we can do everything on our own. But why? Part of it is because the world likes to tell us that dependence equates to weakness—and that if we're weak, we're somehow less valuable. But is that true?

What was the last thing you were dependent on and why?

_____

_____

_____

Dependence is an important characteristic of a branch. Branches of trees are dependent on the tree to stay alive—the moment a branch breaks off the tree, its source of life is removed. The tree in this case represents the "central organization" as described in the definition of *branch* stating, "a separate but dependent part of a central organization."[13]

Our "central organization" is found in Jesus. Paul speaks to the Gentiles about the type of dependency we possess as branches in his letter to the Romans.

> *So then, you must not despise those who were broken off like branches. How can you be proud? You are just a branch; you don't support the roots—the roots support you. Romans 11:18*

Paul makes it clear here that the branch's role is to be supported. In other words, we are dependent on the support of something else. As the vine, Jesus fills the role of the supporter.

In my case, I carried zero dependency on Jesus with me to college. My lack of dependency meant I had to play the role of the *supporter* rather than the *supported*. I placed roots in my new city and in the party scene, and I adapted my lifestyle to support those roots, rather than being rooted in Christ. Each weekend was a new party and talking with a new guy, only to never see each other again because I was too immersed in the party itself to remember his name.

Not surprisingly, my roots didn't grow much. Alcohol doesn't provide quite the same nourishment as compared to the living water God provides. The result of my dependence on alcohol resulted in a lot of emptiness.

How have you been dependent on Jesus?

_____

_____

_____

---

13 *Merriam-Webster's Dictionary and Thesaurus,* Updated Edition, s.v. "Branch."

What happened as a result of your dependence?

_____

_____

_____

_____

_____

It's one thing to know that we should be dependent on Jesus, and it's another to actually depend on him. What benefit does that dependency have? Even though the world likes to say that dependency is a sign of weakness, our weakness does *not* make us less valuable as a person! God says that we are valuable enough to die for and that he will turn our weaknesses into our strengths.

> *For while we were still weak, at the right time Christ died for the ungodly. Romans 5:6 ESV*
> *But he said to me, "My grace is sufficient for you, for my power is made perfect in weakness." Therefore I will boast all the more gladly about my weaknesses, so that Christ's power may rest on me. 2 Corinthians 12:9 NIV*

How can you boast more gladly in your weaknesses?

_____

_____

_____

_____

We all have weaknesses, and that's okay! If we could do everything on our own, we would have no need for Jesus or for the grace he offers.

With that said, I challenge us all to communicate to others that showing weakness does not decrease their value. Our world needs people who encourage others to place their dependence in God, just like we see in the following Psalm:

I depend on God alone; I put my hope in him. He alone protects and saves me; he is my defender, and I shall never be defeated. My salvation and honor depend on God; he is my strong protector; he is my shelter. Trust in God at all times, my people. Tell him all your troubles, for he is our refuge. Psalms 62:5–8

Our honor and salvation depend on God. Jesus is our sole connection to God and our source for salvation. He is the *only* person we can place our dependence on, and he actually means it when he says that we will *never* be defeated. Placing our dependence on Jesus does not make us weak; quite the opposite, it makes us *strong*.

In the midst of my emptiness, I began to evaluate the choice I made to move and establish new roots—was it worth it to stay? I looked to my future and what college would be like if I continued to live the same life. To be honest, it didn't look great. I wasn't sure if I'd ever get the kind of community I wanted. Continuing to depend only on myself, I had some questions to answer; I just wasn't sure what those answers were yet. With the spring term just beginning, I luckily had some time to figure that out.

How could you encourage someone in your life to place their dependence on Jesus?

_____

_____

———————————————————————————

———————————————————————————

———————————————————————————

—m—

Lesson 4: Descendants

At some point in life, we all wonder who we really are and how we got here. Curiosity is an inherent characteristic of human nature. Part of learning where we came from involves exploring an intangible type of tree—a family tree. This desire to know where we came from has exploded over recent years, evidenced by the multiple companies that have emerged to help us find the answer.

In a family tree, branches represent, "a division of a family descended from one ancestor."[14] Just like each of us, Jesus was part of a family tree. The ancestor Jesus's tree descended from, over the course of forty-two generations, was Abraham.

> *So all the generations from Abraham to David were fourteen generations, and from David to the deportation to Babylon fourteen generations, and from the deportation to Babylon to the Christ fourteen generations. Matthew 1:17 ESV*

What is significant about Jesus coming from the line of Abraham? To answer that question, we must look to the following promise God makes with Abraham:

---

14 *Merriam-Webster's Dictionary and Thesaurus,* Updated Edition, s.v. "Branch."

The LORD took him outside and said, "Look at the sky and try to count the stars; you will have as many descendants as that." Genesis 15:5

This promise may have sounded good to Abraham, but at the time, Abraham was almost a hundred years old and had no children. Where were his descendants going to come from? Abraham wondered the same thing.

But Abram said, "Sovereign LORD, what can you give me since I remain childless and the one who will inherit my estate is Eliezer of Damascus?" Genesis 15:2 NIV

Just like Abraham, then known as *Abram*, questioned God, I continued to question myself. What was going to happen if I stayed at the same school for the remainder of college? I had made some good friends, but most of them weren't in fields of study close to mine, and I knew that as we progressed in our college careers, our schedules would drift apart. We would never get to see each other, and any sense of community I thought I had would vanish. I also hadn't gotten deeply involved in any clubs or organizations that would give me a great enough sense of attachment to not be okay with leaving them.

Has God ever told you something that seemed unbelievable or impossible at the time? If so, what was it, and what was the result?

_____

_____

_____

_____

_____

After concluding that I was unlikely to gain the kind of community I wanted in my current environment, I made the decision to move closer to home. I applied to the school I told myself in high school I would never go to, and I transferred there the following semester. I was sad to break the news to my new friends that I was leaving, but I trusted in myself to make the best decision for my future. I made the most of my time with these friends before I left.

On the other hand, Abraham put his trust in God. He had no idea how much God was going to bless him through his son. As promised, God provided him with that son.

> *Sarah became pregnant and bore a son to Abraham in his old age, at the very time God had promised him. Abraham gave the name Isaac to the son Sarah bore him. Genesis 21:2–3 NIV*

Once God fulfilled his promise to Abraham and gave him a son, God took his untraditional ways of fulfilling his promise a step further. God asked Abraham to go and sacrifice his only son—the son God had faithfully provided him.

> *Some time later God tested Abraham. He said to him, "Abraham!" "Here I am," he replied. Then God said, "Take your son, your only son, whom you love—Isaac—and go to the region of Moriah. Sacrifice him there as a burnt offering on a mountain I will show you." Genesis 22:1–2 NIV*

How has God tested you and what were the results?

_____

_____

_____

Along the way to make the burnt offering, Isaac's curiosity surfaced and he wondered exactly what offering they were going to make:

Isaac spoke up and said to his father Abraham, "Father?" "Yes, my son?" Abraham replied. "The fire and wood are here," Isaac said, "but where is the lamb for the burnt offering?" Abraham answered, "God himself will provide the lamb for the burnt offering, my son." And the two of them went on together. Genesis 22:7–8 NIV

I can only imagine what went through Abraham's mind in that moment. Abraham, known as a man with great faith, was fully ready to sacrifice his one and only son in response to his faith in God. He knew that if Isaac wasn't going to be sacrificed, God needed to provide a sacrifice, and that's exactly what happened.

Then he reached out his hand and took the knife to slay his son. But the angel of the LORD called out to him from heaven, "Abraham! Abraham!" "Here I am," he replied. "Do not lay a hand on the boy," he said. "Do not do anything to him. Now I know that you fear God, because you have not withheld from me your son, your only son." Abraham looked up and there in a thicket he saw a ram caught by its horns. He went over and took the ram and sacrificed it as a burnt offering instead of his son. Genesis 22:10–13 NIV

How do you need God to provide for you right now?

_____

_____

_____

_____

God will never ask us to do something he isn't also willing to do. It was God's plan all along to provide the ram for Abraham, just as it was God's plan all along to not withhold his one and only Son from us as a sacrifice for our sins. The ram in the story of Abraham is a foreshadowing to Jesus, who is also known as the Lamb of God.

> *The next day John saw Jesus coming toward him and said, "Look, the Lamb of God, who takes away the sin of the world!" John 1:29 NIV*

In his love for us, God sent Jesus, the Lamb of God, to sacrifice his life in a way none of us ever can to pay for our sins—payment we all deserve to make ourselves.

What prevents you from being willing to give up the things you love for God and his plan for you?

_____

_____

_____

_____

How can you sacrifice what you have currently to better those around you?

_____

_____

_____

_____

Dear God,

Your promise says that all who remain in you will bear much fruit. Your desire is for the fruit I bear to be a blessing to all you have placed in my life. Just as the branch of an apple tree can do nothing unless it stays connected to its tree, I can do nothing unless I stay connected to you. I pray against anything telling me I need to be more like someone else. You created everything and everyone on this earth, and everything you create is good. Help me to know and experience the fullness of being your light by shining to those around me. You are a good Father who desires nothing more than to be my biggest supporter, and you want me to be completely dependent on you. You did not withhold sacrificing your one and only Son for the payment of my sin, and you call me to have the same mentality in not withholding anything I have in order to advance your kingdom. Thank you for being a God who provides, and show me how I can be one who provides for those around me.

In Jesus' name,

Amen.

Chapter Four

THEY ARE WELCOME

Lesson 1: Presence

Suppose you've moved to a new city and are looking for a new church to attend. In order for any new church to give you the impression that it's a place you could see ourselves attending, it is important that you get the experience of a welcoming environment. When you feel welcomed, we feel seen in some way—like our presence matters.

Welcoming others holds such importance, it's often the first thing we want any guest to know. Think about it: what's the mat we place outside our front door called? That's right—it's called a *welcome* mat.

While moving away from my friends I had made during my first year of college wasn't easy, this time around I moved to a place where I already knew people. At the very least, I knew I'd be welcomed by my established friends who lived nearby. What I didn't know was whether anyone at my new school would welcome in this new transfer student in their classes. In my mind, they had already made friends and wouldn't be as intentional in getting to know someone new like they did as freshman.

Name a time when you *did not* feel welcome at a place. What additional feelings did that experience cause you to have about that place and did you ever go back?

_____

_____

_____

_____

_____

Name a time when you *did* feel welcome at a place. What additional feelings did that experience cause you to have about that place and did you ever go back?

_____

_____

_____

_____

_____

> **Welcome:** *adjective* received gladly into one's presence; giving pleasure: pleasing; willingly permitted or admitted[15]

If we treat people in the same way God treats them, we need to be people who welcome others in the same ways Jesus welcomed them.

---

15 *Merriam-Webster's Dictionary and Thesaurus,* Updated Edition, s.v. "Welcome."

Now the tax collectors and sinners were all gathering around to hear Jesus. But the Pharisees and the teachers of the law muttered, "This man welcomes sinners and eats with them." Luke 15:1–2 NIV

Not only does that verse point to how Jesus welcomed people and ate with them, the verse specifically states how he welcomed *sinners*. By doing this, Jesus welcomed a group of people who many refused to acknowledge.

I had no clue what I was doing at the time, but in reality, I identified myself as having the rank of a "sinner or tax collector" before even talking to anyone in my classes. I told myself I was the one they wouldn't want to acknowledge—talk about an unfair assumption!

Those around me proved me wrong. It didn't take long for those in my classes to welcome me into their groups of friends and to continue living out the party life I established the year prior. This time around, most of those friends were in fields of study related to mine.

The way Jesus welcomed the sinners and tax collectors in this time was so revolutionary, that earlier in the book of Luke we see the Pharisees test Jesus by asking him why he would dare do such a thing.

But the Pharisees and the teachers of the law who belonged to their sect complained to his disciples, "Why do you eat and drink with tax collectors and sinners?" Jesus answered them, "It is not the healthy who need a doctor, but the sick. I have not come to call the righteous, but sinners to repentance." Luke 5:30–32 NIV

Why exactly was Jesus so welcoming? Jesus came with an invitation for all people. He welcomes all into his presence, no matter how "sick" they appear. There is no person on this earth that Jesus isn't qualified to heal, and *we* become the people God uses as his hands and feet to bring the news of his healing presence!

How do you welcome those around you?

_____

_____

_____

_____

When we hesitate to welcome others, it's often because welcoming them would cause us difficulty or discomfort in some way. The problem with that hesitation is that God never promised us that following his will would be easy or comfortable. A physician's job would be easy if they spent their entire day seeing nothing but healthy patients. Jesus came to bring healing to the *sick*, and I'm going to guess that Jesus wasn't very comfortable while he died on the cross for our sins so he could bring us the source for our healing.

What in your life prevents you from welcoming everyone around you?

_____

_____

_____

_____

Who is someone in your life you need to be more welcoming to and why?

_____

_____

_____

—ᗰ—

Lesson 2: Gladness

In order to be people who truly understand what it means to welcome others, we need to know how to receive. As stated in the definition, "receiving gladly into one's presence,"[16] indicates that receiving is a fundamental part of welcoming others.

Any time we walk into an environment, it takes us less than five seconds to determine whether others there welcome our presence. We immediately analyze our environment. Did someone come to greet us? What facial expressions do people have when they see us?

To receive the presence of others requires an action on our end. The type of action we take—or the way in which we receive others—is a key factor for communicating to others that they are welcome. If we receive their presence with actions of resentment, they will not have the experience of being welcomed.

What does the concept of being receptive of others mean to you?

_____

_____

_____

In what ways do you show those around you that you are receptive of them?

_____

_____

_____

---

16 *Merriam-Webster's Dictionary and Thesaurus,* Updated Edition, s.v. "Welcome."

Instead, if we want people to feel welcome in our presence, our actions must be done out of *gladness*. We can see an example of receiving the presence of someone gladly in the following interaction between Jesus and Zacchaeus:

> *Jesus entered Jericho and was passing through. A man was there by the name of Zacchaeus; he was a chief tax collector and was wealthy. He wanted to see who Jesus was, but because he was short he could not see over the crowd. So he ran ahead and climbed a sycamore-fig tree to see him, since Jesus was coming that way. When Jesus reached the spot, he looked up and said to him, "Zacchaeus, come down immediately. I must stay at your house today." So he came down at once and welcomed him gladly. Luke 19:1–6 NIV*

When Jesus asked to stay at Zacchaeus's house, Zacchaeus "welcomed him gladly." In another version, that same verse states, *"So he hurried and came down and received him joyfully." Luke 19:6 ESV*

These two different versions highlight both a correlation between welcoming those around us and the way in which we receive their presence.

Jesus showed great intentionality in wanting to stay at Zacchaeus's house. Zacchaeus held the title of "chief tax collector." In those times, people didn't think highly of or welcome tax collectors. However, Zacchaeus wasn't just an average tax collector; Luke specifically states that Zacchaeus was a *chief* tax collector and was *wealthy*. There is a good chance Zacchaeus gained his wealth by unfairly taking a lot of money from people, and it's likely that the community hated him a bit more than they would an "average" tax collector.

Despite Jesus knowing exactly who Zacchaeus was, Jesus wasted *no time* in welcoming him into his presence. As soon as Jesus reached the tree Zacchaeus sat in, Jesus asked him to come down immediately. Zacchaeus reciprocated the gesture by coming down to Jesus at once and welcoming Jesus into his house "gladly" and "joyfully" as the two versions indicate.

Receiving others into our presence gladly means to do so with joy.

Glad: *adjective* characterized by or showing cheerfulness, joy, or pleasure, as looks or utterances[17]

Think of a time when someone received you into their presence gladly or with joy; how did their actions make you feel welcome?

_____

_____

_____

_____

_____

Between all the friends I made at my new school and my childhood friends nearby, I had many more places where my presence was welcomed gladly than ever before. In addition to the added level of comfort I felt by being welcome, I got better at welcoming others who were in my presence. Feeling more welcome also meant partying in regular environments rather than a new environment each weekend. I still conversed mostly with men at these parties, but most were guys I knew and not ones whose names I'd forget.

Up to this point in my life, I was very socially cautious. Unless we were already good friends or I had consumed enough alcohol to "loosen up" my lack of social confidence, being the first one to stir up conversation and making sure everyone around me felt welcome wasn't a role I played often.

Learning to welcome those around me gladly came as a result of much practice during the months before I started attending my new

17 *Dictionary.com,* s.v. "Glad," accessed June 27, 2020, https://www.dictionary.com/

school. I spent that summer doing door-to-door sales. If I couldn't make others feel welcome in my presence, then I didn't make any money. During that summer, I capitalized on hundreds of opportunities each week to start conversations with people, and I quickly realized my talent for welcoming others. In a matter of a few weeks I became one of the top sellers in the region.

Since that time, I have learned how including others and making them feel welcome comes very naturally to me and is one of my top strengths. Knowing this now, it comes as no surprise to me that the enemy did everything he could to keep me relatively silent, and it worked for the first two decades of my life. Satan *hates* it when we operate in our strengths, and he does everything he can to silence us!

Zacchaeus, with his identity as a tax collector, likely didn't have giving others the experience of feeling gladly welcomed on his list of perceived strengths. After he accepted Jesus's invitation and welcomed Jesus into his house with gladness, Jesus changed his heart and the atmosphere shifted. The passage continues by saying:

> *All the people saw this and began to mutter, "He has gone to be the guest of a sinner." But Zacchaeus stood up and said to the Lord, "Look, Lord! Here and now I give half of my possessions to the poor, and if I have cheated anybody out of anything, I will pay back four times the amount." Jesus said to him, "Today salvation has come to this house, because this man, too, is a son of Abraham. For the Son of Man came to seek and to save the lost." Luke 19:7–10 NIV*

Immediately after Zacchaeus welcomed Jesus into his home, several responses took place. First was the judgment of those watching, who gave Zacchaeus the label of a sinner and who judged Jesus for wanting to be the guest of a sinner.

Next came the response from Zacchaeus. Once Zacchaeus welcomed Jesus into his home, his entire demeanor changed. He went from a wealthy tax collector who took money from people, to someone who desired to share his wealth with the poor and to pay back all he had cheated. Jesus then followed up Zacchaeus's response by saying that salvation had been brought to his home. Zacchaeus was no longer lost, but found!

Just like he did with Zacchaeus, Jesus came to earth to save *all* who are lost:

> *For I am not ashamed of the gospel, because it is the power of God that brings salvation to everyone who believes: first to the Jew, then to the Gentile. Romans 1:16 NIV*

The debt for our sins has been paid! When we welcome Jesus into our lives and receive his punishment for our sins, we are no longer looked on as sinners, but as people who are saved—holy and blameless. Accepting Jesus's payment for our sins frees us up to extend that same grace and joyfully welcome those around us.

How has gladly receiving Jesus into your presence changed you?

_____

_____

_____

In what ways could you give to others and welcome them into your presence as a response of joy?

_____

_____

_____

—〽—

Lesson 3: Pleasure

Over the course of the past few years, Chick-fil-A® has single-handedly changed the culture of service expectations within the fast food industry. One of the main reasons for that culture shift is due to the way in which they treat and welcome their customers. When a customer orders, a staff member commonly replies, "My pleasure." This gesture seems simple, but it has brought significant enough change that competitors can't help but notice. Behavior like this perfectly embodies the aspect of welcoming others as seen in the definition, "giving pleasure."[18]

<u>**Pleasure:**</u> *noun* a source of delight or joy[19]

When we introduce ourselves, people often respond by saying something like, "It is a *pleasure* to meet you." In other words, our presence brought them pleasure. Looking to the definition of *pleasure* we see the word *source*. When we experience pleasure, it becomes the source for us to harbor both delight and joy.

How different would our world look if we intentionally gave pleasure and welcomed people everywhere we went? One thing is for certain, we would see significantly more joy in the world than we do today. If that alone isn't enough, I'm not sure what is.

Showing pleasure allows us to be people who welcome others in the way God does when he takes pleasure in us. We are *not* just a number to God!

For the LORD takes pleasure in his people; he adorns the humble with salvation. Psalms 149:4 ESV

---

18   *Merriam-Webster's Dictionary and Thesaurus,* Updated Edition, s.v. "Welcome."
19   *Merriam-Webster's Dictionary and Thesaurus,* Updated Edition, s.v. "Pleasure."

If someone had asked me at this point in my college life, "Do you think God takes pleasure in you?" my quick response would have been "No." What was there to take pleasure in? I figured I had to give God—and everyone else for that matter—a reason to be pleased with me. Feeling welcome in this capacity went beyond my understanding.

With delight and joy coming as products of giving pleasure, welcoming others by showing gladness and joy comes easily when we surround ourselves with people who are "pleasing" to be around. Now, this isn't me trying to say we are taking the easy way out if we surround ourselves with people who are pleasing to be around. The people we find pleasing to be around are likely our closest and most trusted friends or family, and showing joy or being around those people are not bad things. Having close community is of utmost importance to God.

What it *does* mean is that if we want to be people who welcome others by giving pleasure to those around us, it might not always be easy. In fact, doing so requires a greater level of intentionality from us. Our welcoming them must come from a place of us desiring to give *them* a joyful experience, not because they give *us* a joyful experience.

How do we facilitate a lifestyle of giving pleasure to those around us? God gives us a few examples in qualities he finds pleasing:

Loyalty: *Never let go of loyalty and faithfulness. Tie them around your neck; write them on your heart. If you do this, both God and people will be pleased with you. Proverbs 3:3–4*

Integrity: *I know that you test everyone's heart and are pleased with people of integrity. In honesty and sincerity I have willingly given all this to you, and I have seen how your people who are gathered here have been happy to bring offerings to you. 1 Chronicles 29:17*

Goodness: *Do not forget to do good and to help one another, because these are the sacrifices that please God. Hebrews 13:16*

When have you made those around you feel welcome through your extension of loyalty, integrity, or goodness?

_____

_____

_____

_____

_____

When have others made you feel welcome by showing loyalty, integrity, or goodness to you?

_____

_____

_____

_____

_____

How have you felt God's pleasure as a result of having loyalty, integrity, or goodness?

_____

_____

_____

_____

_____

Possessing the qualities of loyalty, integrity, and goodness have always been important to me. I have never been a good liar and I highly value being there for my friends in any way I can. Yet, despite living out these qualities to the best of my ability, I did so because I felt it was right, not because I was intentional about giving those around me the experience of being welcome.

My loyalty spread to multiple groups of friends, and as a result I found myself getting drunk at parties three or four nights a week. In the midst of my drunkenness, I certainly found delight by being in their presence. The effects of the drinking, however, were far from delightful. I don't see God ever saying that he finds getting drunk to be a pleasing activity—because it isn't pleasing.

I also held up my integrity in my relationships with men. I had no interest in having sex with anyone who wasn't husband material, and I stuck to that, even if it brought an experience opposite of delight to a few men. Sure, it probably would have given them pleasure, but not the kind of pleasure associated with making others feel welcome. That's not all: it would have cost me my integrity in the process.

Although we are called to show loyalty, integrity, and goodness to those around us, what ultimately pleases God is our faith.

And without faith it is impossible to please God, because anyone who comes to him must believe that he exists and that he rewards those who earnestly seek him. Hebrews 11:6 NIV

Don't get me wrong—showing loyalty, integrity, and goodness toward God are integral parts to living in the fullness of the relationship God wants us to have with him. At the end of the day, if we do each of those things and fail to have faith in God and *his* goodness, we've missed the point.

It is our faith—our belief that God exists and that Jesus died to pay the price for our sins—that allows us to be welcome into heaven. God never asks us to do something that pleases him without also guaranteeing pleasure on his end too.

Do not conform to the pattern of this world, but be transformed by the renewing of your mind. Then you will be able to test and approve what God's will is—his good, pleasing and perfect will. Romans 12:2 NIV

It takes faith to live out God's will for our life. His will is good, pleasing and perfect. The invitation to live out God's will for our life, rather than our own, is always on the table; all we need to do is earnestly seek it.

How has God rewarded you in your faith?

_____

_____

_____

_____

What prevents you from earnestly seeking God daily?

_____

_____

_____

_____

—〰—

Lesson 4: Willingness

At some point in life, every one of us has received an invitation to an event. Regardless of the event's nature—whether it's a family function, a school dance, or a wedding—inviting guests is a key component to the organization of that event. When it comes to feeling welcome at an event, receiving an invitation to it only tells part of the story. Looking into the definition of welcome— "willingly permitted or admitted,"[20]—is the other key to helping us feel welcome.

We see that just being invited—or in other words, permitted—to an event isn't enough. Sometimes we get invited by a friend to a party, and if our friend isn't the one organizing the party, our initial thought could be, "Are you *sure* it's okay if I go with you?" Other times, we get invited to an event out of what we feel is an obligation, and depending on our relationship with the person who invited us, we won't actually feel welcome at their event. Either way, if we don't have the experience of being *willingly* permitted to attend an event, we won't feel welcome.

Can you think of a time when you attended an event where you felt unwelcome even though you were invited? What was it that caused you to feel unwelcome?

_____

_____

_____

_____

_____

How do we show willingness?

Willing: *adjective* done, borne, or accepted voluntarily or without reluctance[21]

In the context of welcoming those around us, accepting their presence without reluctance is crucial. As much as we like to think we can cover

20   *Merriam-Webster's Dictionary and Thesaurus,* Updated Edition, s.v. "Welcome."
21   *Merriam-Webster's Dictionary and Thesaurus,* Updated Edition, s.v. "Willing."

up our reluctance, we can't. People can see right through us when we reluctantly accept their presence.

How, then, can we show our willingness? The Bible calls us to show our willingness in the forms of:

> <u>Listening</u>: *A warning given by an experienced person to someone willing to listen is more valuable than gold rings or jewelry made of the finest gold. Proverbs 25:12*
>
> <u>Learning</u>: *If you listen to advice and are willing to learn, one day you will be wise. Proverbs 19:20*
>
> <u>Working</u>: *For even when we were with you, we would give you this command: If anyone is not willing to work, let him not eat. 2 Thessalonians 3:10 ESV*

How has your willingness to listen, learn, or work allowed someone else to feel welcome in your presence?

_____

_____

_____

_____

_____

How has someone else's willingness to listen, learn, or work allowed you to feel welcome in their presence?

_____

_____

_____

_____

How different would our world be if we were all willing to listen to those around us, learn from our mistakes, and work to contribute to society? My guess is that a lot more people would feel welcome in their everyday environments.

As I formed deeper relationships with the people I met in my new everyday environment, the number of times someone willingly invited me somewhere became more frequent. Being someone who highly values making sure people feel included, it felt nice to have the inclusion reciprocated. Things seemed to be looking up in my decision to move and in my deeper search for unity, and I was willing to learn and work as hard as I needed to in order to achieve it.

God also has a character of willingness. No one wants to welcome us into their presence more than him, and he willingly gave us his all to reunite us with him. God expresses his commitment by being willing to:

Save Us: *Israel, trust in the LORD, because his love is constant and he is always willing to save. Psalms 130:7*
Die for Us: *I am the good shepherd. As the Father knows me and I know the Father, in the same way I know my sheep and they know me. And I am willing to die for them. John 10:14–15*

Talk about the best news the world has ever heard! God is *always* willing to save us, and he did just that by sending Jesus, who willingly died to pay the price for our sins.

Think about it: how different would our view of Jesus dying on the cross for our sins look if the only reason he died was because he felt obligated to? I'm guessing none of us would feel quite as *welcome* in his presence if that were the case.

The good news for us is that's not how the story took place. The truth is that Jesus *willingly* died for our sins because God doesn't want us to be separated from him. God wants nothing more than to welcome us into his presence for all of eternity in heaven.

How have God's love and sacrifice for you allowed you to feel welcome in his presence?

_____

_____

_____

_____

_____

What can you do to further place your trust in God and his willingness to always save you?

_____

_____

_____

_____

_____

—〰—

Dear God,

You are a God who goes out of your way to welcome all, including those our world says we should cast out. Feeling welcome is an essential element to building relationships, and you are always there waiting to gladly receive my presence when I make the choice to build my relationship with you. I confess that I don't always receive the presence of those around me gladly or joyfully. I wish to live my life in a way that is unashamed of the gospel—in a way that the people in this world would know I welcome them because of having been changed by your radical love. Reveal to me areas of my life that lack loyalty, integrity, or goodness, so that I may live in a way more aligned with your good and pleasing will for my life. I acknowledge that in order to truly make people feel welcome, I must welcome them willingly and not out of obligation. Thank you for always being willing to save me and for sending Jesus to die for my sins. I open myself to be more willing to listen to, learn from, and work for the goodness of your kingdom, because you want nothing more than to welcome me into your presence for all eternity.

In Jesus' name,

Amen.

Chapter Five

THEY BELONG

Lesson 1: Suitable

We learn about the concept of belonging very early in life. As soon as we become old enough to walk and talk, we begin to make friends and search for our sense of belonging. Conveying the message to someone that they belong is often done in an abstract manner, through the implication of our words or actions.

Every day, people are in environments where they feel they don't truly belong. For example, if we sit in a room and think everyone there is smarter than us, we may think we don't belong. And, if we feel like we haven't been a "good enough" person, we may not think we belong at church. While our thought of not belonging in either of those situations isn't true, that doesn't invalidate the experience, or feeling, of not belonging.

For the first time in my life, I reached a point where I gained a sense of belonging through my own social initiative. Others welcomed my presence, and I thought I was on track to getting what I hoped to achieve by transferring to a new school. After all, having a place of belonging has its benefits. I felt wanted, and that feeling convinced me that I both mattered and had worth.

The issue was, my feeling of belonging stemmed from an unhealthy source, and my belonging came at an unsustainable cost to myself. The cost wasn't monetary, but it was physical and emotional. Unfortunately, I remained blind to the cost for the first months. It wasn't much to pay on any individual night, so I remained willing to pay it.

When was a time you felt you *did not* belong somewhere and how did it make you feel?

_____

_____

_____

_____

_____

When was a time you felt you *did* belong somewhere and how did it make you feel?

_____

_____

_____

_____

_____

The isolation that comes from feeling like we don't belong is real, deep, and lonely. Satan loves nothing more than to tell every single one of us that we don't belong here. When we experience the feeling that we don't belong, it creates an environment for division.

It is extremely important that we see others as having a place of belonging. How can we be the type of people who shift our culture and communicate to those around us that they belong?

Belong: *verb* to be suitable or appropriate; to be attached (as through birth or membership); to form an attribute or part; to be classified[22]

This first lesson addresses one of the more common ways of determining a sense of belonging, which is when we determine that something is "suitable or appropriate." From job interviews, to elections and first impressions, we make judgments every day on whether people are suitable for certain places or jobs.

My experience was no different. As time in my new communities progressed, the pressure to maintain a sense of belonging increased in a subtle and gradual manner both in and out of the classroom. Despite getting along with my classmates well, I knew I didn't belong in my engineering classes. One could say thermodynamics isn't exactly my life's passion. Transferring schools left me behind in the engineering classes I was supposed to be in with others in my same year, which certainly didn't help give me a sense of being suitable.

Once class dismissed and the partying began, the pressure to belong didn't dissipate. My ability to drink large quantities came with a reputation and the friendships I formed began to form unspoken expectations along with them. Balancing this developed reputation left an impression on those

---

22 *Merriam-Webster's Dictionary and Thesaurus,* Updated Edition, s.v. "Belong."

around me; it also gave me something to live up to as far as having a place to belong goes. For the time being, I lived up to it fairly well, so my sense of belonging remained.

Although it is true that we each have a unique set of life experiences that make us more suitable in certain roles or environments than others, for the purpose of this chapter we will look at belonging from a more global aspect. God created and brought everyone on earth for a specific purpose. Anything that tells us we don't belong here is *not from God*! Having a sense of belonging is in the very nature of how God created us.

> *Then the LORD God said, "It is not good for the man to live alone. I will make a suitable companion to help him." Genesis 2:18*

Not only did Eve belong simply because God made her, but also because God had a specific purpose for her. If someone else told Eve that she didn't belong there—and caused her to leave as a result—Adam would have been affected as well.

Eve wasn't a suitable companion for Adam because of anything she did or because of a quality she possessed. Eve was a suitable companion for Adam because God said she was suitable—it's as simple as that!

If we base our sense of belonging here on anything other than the fact that it's in the nature of how God created us, we will find ourselves falling short of our expectations every single time. God made each of us unique to every other person on this planet. No one has the same combination of gifts, talents, upbringing, and experiences as we do. What we all *do* have in common is that the *same* God created us.

It wasn't good for Adam to be alone, and it isn't good for us to be alone either. None of us was brought here by accident; we are all suitably qualified to fulfill the purpose God gave us. God desires nothing more than for us to develop a relationship with him so that we can live in the fullness of our purpose.

When was a time you *did* feel suitably qualified? Did those feelings give you a sense of belonging?

_____

_____

_____

_____

_____

When was a time you *did not* feel suitably qualified? Did those feelings take away from your sense of belonging?

_____

_____

_____

_____

How does your belonging impact those around you?

_____

_____

_____

_____

—∿—

Lesson 2: Attached

Determining whether something or someone belongs can be done many different ways. One figurative way is having an overall feeling or experience of belonging. Another, more literal, aspect is seen in the definition "to be attached (as through birth or membership)."[23]

Attachment in this definition comes from two different sources—birth and membership. Both birth and membership are concepts common to our life on earth. As for birth, each of us on this planet was brought here through birth. Anything telling us that we don't belong on earth is a lie!

As far as memberships are concerned, the world contains many organizations we can either become a member of or belong to. Early on in my new environment, I helped grow my sense of belonging by gaining membership to an organization and learning ballroom dancing. I never took to any kind of dance before, but I enjoyed learning something new. The others involved furthered my sense of belonging by teaching me all of the dances, starting with the basics.

No one that I grew up with believed me in the slightest when I told them I joined the ballroom dance team—it was way too "girly" an activity. Nevertheless, I joined, and I began to love it. For someone who had never seen herself as a dancer, ballroom dancing is highly linear and methodical, lending itself well to my mathematically wired brain.

Has your membership in an organization ever given you a sense of belonging? If so, how?

_____

_____

_____

_____

_____

23 *Merriam-Webster's Dictionary and Thesaurus,* Updated Edition, s.v. "Belong."

Belonging by means of birth and membership don't apply only in an earthly sense. They are also demonstrated in the body of Christ.

> **Birth:** *Blessed be the God and Father of our Lord Jesus Christ! According to his great mercy, he has caused us to be born again to a living hope through the resurrection of Jesus Christ from the dead, to an inheritance that is imperishable, undefiled, and unfading, kept in heaven for you, who by God's power are being guarded through faith for a salvation ready to be revealed in the last time. 1 Peter 1:3–5 ESV*
> **Membership:** *For as in one body we have many members, and the members do not all have the same function, so we, though many, are one body in Christ, and individually members of one another. Romans 12:4–5 ESV*

I love the way that birth and membership are addressed in those verses, because they radically shift the way we view what it means to belong. The shift comes in the reason through which we are born again—God's mercy.

When was a time that you were blessed by God's mercy?

_____

_____

_____

Do you consider yourself as being born into or a member of the body of Christ? If so, has that given you a sense of belonging? Why or why not?

_____

_____

_____

I had little knowledge of the concept of mercy at this time in my life, and it showed in my pursuit to maintain a sense of belonging. Not only did I feel my own weight of trying to maintain this sense of belonging, I also took on the responsibility of giving others the experience of belonging. Giving others the experience of belonging can be a great thing for others if done in a healthy way. After all, God designed us with the need to be connected.

Giving the experience of belonging can also be done in unhealthy ways, and I began to see this play itself out in my life. I set lofty expectations for myself by placing responsibility for other's feelings of belonging onto myself. In addition to those lofty expectations, I gave myself little mercy during the process—talk about an environment perfect for stirring up the experience of being a failure time and time again!

The great news when it comes to God is that our belonging isn't even in question. When it comes to being a part of the body of Christ, belonging is an inherent characteristic of all who are a part of the body. Every person in the body of Christ connects to one another. Each part belongs, and each has its designated purpose. There is no person on this planet to whom God isn't willing to extend mercy. Everyone who receives God's mercy and is born again then becomes a member of the body of Christ.

The truth is, none of us by our actions alone even deserve access to the imperishable, undefiled, and unfading inheritance that comes as a result of being born again. Only by God's mercy do we get access to the inheritance that comes from being born into the resurrection of Christ. God *wants* to share his inheritance with us, and if that isn't amazing, I don't know what is!

What prevents you from extending mercy to those around you?

_____

_____

_____

How can you extend mercy to someone in a current life situation?

_____

_____

_____

_____

_____

—ɯɯ—

Lesson 3: Attribute

The process of deciding whether something belongs based on its attributes is one we are taught at a very young age. These attributes can be concrete, such as kids not belonging in bars due to their age. They can also be abstract, like the great debate of whether pineapple belongs on pizza. (For the record, it's not my favorite, but I don't think it's that bad.)

Our society today places an extremely high value on wanting all our attributes to be accepted. We want to know that we play a part in belonging during our time on earth.

How have any of your attributes given you the experience that you _do not_ belong somewhere?

_____

_____

_____

_____

_____

**How have any of your attributes given you the experience that you
do belong somewhere?**

_____

_____

_____

_____

_____

The decision of whether something belongs somewhere comes by
means of a judgment. The question is, who gets to be the judge? When we
allow the ways of this world to judge our belonging, we experience feelings
of inadequacy or insufficiency.

I allowed others' judgments of my attributes to strongly influence
my overall sense of belonging for too long. Although I still searched for
belonging in relationships, I shifted away from talking to different men
at parties each week and toward pursuing a more long-term relationship.
When I made that shift, people started to become very interested in learning
more about my attributes and the attributes of those I'd be interested in
having a relationship with.

I didn't date much before college, so this was fairly new territory. I
began to feel pressure in ways I never felt before. The world became much
more curious about how my conversations with men went and if "anything
had happened." I kept my boundary of not being sexually active during this
time, but the expectations of the world were getting to me.

To say feelings of inadequacy and insufficiency arose would be an
understatement. I longed for a deep sense of connection and unity, and
I increased how much I worked to achieve it. My increase in effort
didn't translate successfully into the results I looked for. This created
the perfect environment to breed daily thoughts of inadequacy and
insufficiency.

People in the Bible also dealt with feelings of inadequacy, as we see in this passage where God interacts with Moses:

"So now, go. I am sending you to Pharaoh to bring my people the Israelites out of Egypt." But Moses said to God, "Who am I that I should go to Pharaoh and bring the Israelites out of Egypt?" And God said, "I will be with you. And this will be the sign to you that it is I who have sent you: When you have brought the people out of Egypt, you will worship God on this mountain." Moses said to God, "Suppose I go to the Israelites and say to them, 'The God of your fathers has sent me to you,' and they ask me, 'What is his name?' Then what shall I tell them?" God said to Moses, "I AM WHO I AM. This is what you are to say to the Israelites: 'I AM has sent me to you.'" Exodus 3:10–14 NIV

The conversation in this passage takes place as God appeared to Moses in the burning bush and called Moses to bring the Israelites out of Egypt. Moses's reaction to the call? He *immediately* doubted his belonging in the situation by starting his response to God with the words, *Who am I?*

Even though Moses didn't see himself as belonging in the calling God gave him, God did. At the end of the day, God wouldn't call any of us into something if he didn't plan on providing us with the attributes necessary to succeed.

I thought I knew what I wanted in a romantic relationship, but I began to feel more and more like I didn't. Doubt crept in, and the external pressure I felt didn't help. Externally, I belonged. Internally, the energy it took to achieve that belonging took its toll on me. Taking on the weight of responsibility for other people's feeling of belonging only added to my exhaustion. Unlike Moses, I did not take my doubt to God.

God wasn't surprised by Moses's doubt, and he isn't surprised by ours either. It's okay for us to take our doubt to him. When God calls us to a place, nothing else has authority to tell us we don't belong there.

Have you ever been called to something and had a reaction similar to Moses by thinking, *Who am I?* What was the calling and how did it result?

_____

_____

_____

_____

_____

God responded to Moses's doubt by assuring Moses that he would be with Moses. How can you assure someone else that God is with them?

_____

_____

_____

_____

_____

—m—

Lesson 4: Classification

If you searched the classifieds section on a news site, you would find people looking to both buy and sell all kinds of products and services. One of the reasons these pages are successful is because they group items in categories, and you can search for an item by picking the category the item belongs to. As seen in the last definition of *belong* ("to be classified") the word *classify* means:

<u>**Classify:**</u> *verb* to consider (someone or something) as belonging to a particular group[24]

When it comes to inanimate objects, classification is a pretty straightforward process. How does that change when it comes to classifying people?

What do you classify yourself as?

_____

_____

_____

_____

_____

Where do you feel like you belong because of that classification?

_____

_____

_____

_____

_____

Making those classifications of others isn't in itself a bad thing to do. But if we're honest with ourselves, we've all made false classifications of others—that's just human nature. Although our classification of others is not going to magically stop, we can control what we do with those classifications. Just because we classify someone as belonging to a group to which we don't belong to, we have no right to consider them less valuable

---

24 *Merriam-Webster.com*, s.v. "Classify," accessed June 28, 2020, https://www.merriam-webster.com/

as a person. The Bible is clear in saying that we are to consider others above ourselves:

> *Don't do anything from selfish ambition or from a cheap desire to boast, but be humble toward one another, always considering others better than yourselves. And look out for one another's interests, not just for your own. Philippians 2:3–4*

Who have you not been considering as better than yourself, and how can you take a step toward doing so?

_____

_____

_____

_____

Notice that the verse in Philippians does not say that we lack value. Quite the opposite: if everyone in society valued everyone above themselves, *all* of us would benefit as a result. God knows just how much we would benefit from that, and he would never ask us to do something that he doesn't also do himself.

> *You see, at just the right time, when we were still powerless, Christ died for the ungodly. Romans 5:6 NIV*

Who exactly are the "ungodly"? As part of his nature, God is without sin. Therefore, the ungodly includes all those on earth who have ever committed at least one sin in their life—and since no one is perfect, that includes all of us.

By dying for us, Jesus not only considered our value as higher than his own, he looked to our interests rather than his. When we create an environment where others know that their value is considered and their interests are seen, we give them the experience of having a place where they belong.

Even though I had found a great "earthly" sense of belonging, I became tired of not getting the results I really wanted from all the work I was putting in. Rather than continue down this path of insanity that failed me night after night, I began to withdraw.

My withdrawal came from a place of wanting to figure out how to better sustain my relationships for the long term. I knew I couldn't better sustain my current relationships while remaining immersed in the lifestyle I'd adopted, so I withdrew instead. This decision didn't come with the intention of burning bridges with anyone. I had no desire to change the direction my path headed, but I knew I needed some rest.

I suppose one could say I attempted to live out that passage in Philippians. After all, my decision partially came from a place of wanting to look after the interests of others. The part of my decision that didn't line up with the Philippians passage was that I selfishly did not want to radically change my own life to accomplish those results. Nevertheless, it was a good start, especially given the fact that I didn't consult God directly with any of my problems at this point in life. At the very least, I was on my way to getting to that "right" time where I would truly understand what Romans 5:6 means when saying that it was while we were *powerless* that Christ died for us.

How has someone else given you the experience of belonging somewhere as a result of them considering your value or seeing your interests?

_____

_____

_____

How could you share the interests of someone else in your life to give them the experience of belonging?

_____

_____

_____

_____

_____

—ɱ—

Dear God,

Thank you for being a God who meets my every need—including my need for having a sense of belonging. Being suitably qualified for the twists and turns life throws my way is in the very nature of how you created me and everyone around me. Anything that tells me I don't belong in this world is not from you. You bring us all to this earth by means of birth, and you welcome all who desire to be a part of your body. You have given me all the necessary attributes needed to succeed in all of what you call me to. Remove any areas of doubt I have about my own sense of belonging, and help me to be the kind of person who helps others to see their belonging. I confess that I don't always consider other people's interests above my own, and I ask for your eyes to see an opportunity to do so. You are the perfect example of how to consider someone else's interests above my own, and I am forever grateful that you are a God who is willing to die for me even in my powerlessness.

In Jesus' name,

Amen.

Chapter Six

THEY ARE RESPECTED

Lesson 1: Refrain

The theme of this chapter is one the world values highly: everyone wants respect. While the desire to be respected is a healthy desire, respect can easily be communicated in very unhealthy ways. If we aren't mindful of the way we communicate respect, the message quickly goes from one of treating everyone with love and fairness to one of an unhealthy designation of power. For the purpose of this book and in sticking to the theme of how God sees people, we will stick to the type of respect that includes treating everyone with the same love and fairness.

Respect: *verb* to refrain from interfering with; admire; appreciate; regard[25]

---

25 *Merriam-Webster's Dictionary and Thesaurus,* Updated Edition, s.v. "Respect."

One of the first words in this definition of "respect" is *refrain*. What exactly does refraining from interfering with a situation have to do with respect? In this way, our display of respecting someone comes not by the actions we take toward them, but rather the actions we *don't* take. How can we be people who consciously show this kind of respect to others?

In what ways have you shown respect to others by refraining from interfering with them?

_____

_____

_____

_____

How have you felt *respected* by someone because they refrained from interfering with you?

_____

_____

_____

_____

How have you felt *disrespected* by someone because of their lack of refrain?

_____

_____

_____

Showing respect in this manner sat in the forefront of my mind when I decided to withdraw from certain places and relationships. I knew I didn't like the direction my life was heading in, and I knew something needed to change. I also knew that those other people were just fine with the way things were—they did not see the same need for change.

If I decided to continue life as is, I was disrespecting my future self and the other people in my circle of influence. I tried to figure out how my life had gotten to where it was—a place of a lot of perceived welcome-ness and belonging, but at the same time a place absent of true satisfaction and fulfillment. In no way did I consider myself an expert at communicating love and fairness at this point in my life, but what I did know was that it wasn't fair to me or other people around me for me to continue to live life in this unsatisfactory way.

To be honest, communicating strongly emotional topics has always been hard for me. It's something I still work to improve on daily because of how important I think it is to show respect to others. As a highly action-driven person, showing respect can be even harder to do through the act of refraining. However, the Bible illustrates a few different ways to show refrain.

On behalf of this man I will boast, but on my own behalf I will not boast, except of my weaknesses. Though if I should wish to boast, I would not be a fool, for I would be speaking the truth. But I refrain from it, so that no one may think more of me than he sees in me or hears from me. 2 Corinthians 12:5–6 ESV

Refrain from anger and turn from wrath; do not fret—it leads only to evil. For those who are evil will be destroyed, but those who hope in the LORD will inherit the land. Psalms 37:8–9 NIV

In these examples, we see how respect is shown through the acts of refraining from both anger and boasting. In the case of boasting, Paul respects the value of others around him by choosing not to boast about himself. In the case of anger, respect was shown by not taking an action that would lead only to evil.

Looking at both situations, we easily see the benefits of showing refrain. Notice how even though it might be easy to *see* the benefit of showing refrain, it doesn't necessarily translate into an ease of *showing* refrain. Why is that?

I quickly came to this dilemma in my own situation. Seeing the *benefit* of showing refrain in certain relationships was a piece of cake, but showing the refrain itself was difficult. The weight and stress built up in the life I pursued crushed me, but so did refraining from that life—it didn't make sense.

With each of those passages, the act of showing refrain required valuing the other person above ourselves. What happens if we don't show refrain? We could boast about ourselves—and we may have plenty to boast about—but where would boasting get us if people see we only care about ourselves and our own accomplishments? We could also show anger—and we may have every right to be angry—but where is acting out on our anger going to get us? Not very far, that's where.

I spent many hours in my season of refrain brainstorming how I could return to the life I had while getting a different result. That exercise allowed me to draw closer in some relationships because I got to a place where I communicated more vulnerably. I became tired of trying to convince myself I could figure it out on my own. In my increased vulnerability, I seemed to be gaining more unity in my friendship circles, but the unity didn't come with the people I originally aimed to show respect through my refrain, which meant I still had more to figure out.

How have you shown respect by refraining from showing anger or from boasting?

_____

_____

_____

_____

_____

How have you felt respected by someone else who refrained from showing anger toward you or boasting even if they had good reason to boast or get angry?

_____

_____

_____

_____

—m—

Lesson 2: Admiration

I'll be honest: in thinking about what it means to respect someone, the word *admire* isn't one that originally came to my mind. The power of admiration is one I feel our society waters down too much, to the point that a lot of our admiration is kept secret. Think about it: how many of us had secret admirers at some point in grade school?

While talking about secret admirers in grade school may sound like a silly example, I believe there is a real issue behind the fact that our culture loves to keep admiration secret. It's almost like we're afraid to let people know what we admire—or in other words, respect—about them. But why? To address this question, let's first look at what it means to admire:

Admire: *verb* to regard with wonder, pleasure, or approval[26]

What is something you admire about someone else and why?

_____

_____

_____

_____

_____

Have you ever told that person what you admire about them? Why or why not?

_____

_____

_____

_____

_____

In the definition of *admire* the word that sticks out to me the most is *wonder*. What does it mean to regard something with wonder? Thinking about "wonder" from a worldly context, the wonders of this world come in a variety of both natural and man-made varieties. If we stood before any of the wonders of the world, we couldn't help but admire them. Why, then,

---

26 *Dictionary.com,* s.v. "Admire," accessed June 28, 2020, https://www.dictionary.com/

does our mindset change when it comes to showing admiration for others? How can we respect their uniqueness?

The same God who made the wonders of this world made every person who walks the earth and he made us all *wonderfully*.

For you created my inmost being; you knit me together in my mother's womb. I praise you because I am fearfully and wonderfully made; your works are wonderful, I know that full well. Psalms 139:13–14 NIV

What does being fearfully and wonderfully made mean to you?

_____

_____

_____

_____

_____

After stating that God's works are wonderful, David writes, *"I know that full well."* I love the amount of assurance with which David declares that statement. He knows *fully* that God's works are wonderful. As a result of his assurance, he follows up his statement of being wonderfully made with a few verses that show admiration to God.

My frame was not hidden from you when I was made in the secret place, when I was woven together in the depths of the earth. Your eyes saw my unformed body; all the days ordained for me were written in your book before one of them came to be. How precious to me are your thoughts, God! How vast is the sum of them! Were I to count them, they would outnumber the grains of sand—when I awake, I am still with you. Psalms 139:15–18 NIV

David declares in this passage that he is fully seen by God and that God gave him a purpose in advance for all his days on earth. Think about it, how differently would our world look if we simply admired the fact that God wrote a purpose for all the days of our lives?

While I tried to figure out how to regroup my life in a way that made sense, I didn't know that God wrote out a purpose for my life. I made most of my life's decisions based on one of two mindsets: either what I thought I would succeed at or enjoy, or what I felt logically made the most sense and would provide me with the most benefit. Making the decision to study chemical engineering came from knowing that I enjoyed chemistry and that I excelled at math. The decision seemed logical at the time, but it certainly didn't come from a place of knowing what profession best fit my God-given purpose.

Living a life empty of purpose made it easy to continue a lifestyle of partying. Drinking the nights away didn't seem costly because I didn't place a high enough worth on my life. I wouldn't have used the word *wonderful* to describe myself at this time, but I did see myself as valuable enough to think there just had to be something more satisfactory out there. But searching for that "wonderful" life wasn't quite worth giving up the lifestyle I had built over the years.

Even if we don't feel we are wonderful, it doesn't change the fact that God made us *all* wonderfully. Being wonderful is in the very nature of the way God created us, and *nothing* on this earth can take that away from us. God thinks of us so much, that the number of his thoughts outweighs the number of grains of sand. If we truly understood how wonderful God thinks we are, living a life of admiration would come naturally; we wouldn't think twice about it!

With that said, I encourage us all to actively seek out and listen to God's precious thoughts about us. When we know with full assurance that God made us wonderfully, we become free to extend admiration to those around us. We can facilitate a community of people who show respect for each other.

What prevents you from knowing with full assurance that God made you wonderfully?

_____

_____

_____

_____

_____

How can you show respect to someone in your life through showing admiration?

_____

_____

_____

_____

_____

—◊◊◊—

Lesson 3: Appreciation

When it comes to the modern-day workforce, people stay at their jobs for shorter periods of time than ever before. The number of people working thirty years for one employer and then retiring are decreasing. One of the reasons for this trend is appreciation. People want to know their work has purpose. They want to be treated for what they're worth, and they want to be respected. That's not too much to ask, right? At face value it may not seem like a big ask, but if a company stays more concerned about their bottom line than about the people who contribute to it, appreciation could be hard to come by.

What makes displaying appreciation so hard for our world? How do we become people who show others that we appreciate them?

Appreciate: *verb* to value justly; to judge with understanding[27]

Our society *loves* to complicate the process of showing appreciation. We stay so concerned about the "cost" required to show appreciation that we completely ignore the benefit it brings.

If we boil it down, there are a couple of variables that go into expressing appreciation—value and understanding. How we show appreciation to others may look different for each of us, but at the end of the day, we *all* want to be appreciated. We want be seen, known, and understood, and we cannot be people who show appreciation in a genuine manner unless we recognize the worth of others.

Continuing in my season of withdrawal, appreciation wasn't something I came by frequently. Some people did not see the same need for separation as I did, and it created tension. They took the opposite stance, putting renewed energy into being "extra nice" so I would see our relationship differently. To be honest, it just frustrated me.

I knew prior to their renewed efforts that I wasn't understood because of their inability to see that withdrawal was necessary. But now? Now we were also stepping into the territory of not being seen or known. Trust me, it wouldn't have taken much for someone even somewhat close to me during this season of life to see the destruction going on inside. I spent

---

27 *Merriam-Webster's Dictionary and Thesaurus,* Updated Edition, s.v. "Respect."

many nights in anger, isolation, frustration, or tears. For someone to think that someone could just be extra nice and somehow my feelings would just go away seemed crazy to me. Instead, it communicated that people didn't appreciate what I felt was a good and necessary choice.

When was a time when you *did not* feel appreciated? Why?

_____

_____

_____

_____

_____

When was a time when you *did* feel appreciated? Why?

_____

_____

_____

_____

_____

Part of showing appreciation in a genuine manner comes in the form of how we judge—or don't judge—one another. The Bible has no shortage of references to showing judgment and what showing judgment looks like. Here are a couple of them:

> *"Do not pervert justice; do not show partiality to the poor or favoritism to the great, but judge your neighbor fairly." Leviticus 19:15 NIV*
> *Speak up and judge fairly; defend the rights of the poor and needy. Proverbs 31:9 NIV*

In these verses, we see a commonality with the word *fairly*. They tie directly to the other definition of *appreciate* stating "to value justly" as the word *fair* is a synonym to the word *just*.[28]

In order to show appreciation to others, we need to be aware of how we judge them and see their value. God values every single person on earth equally, and as a result, he always shows appreciation through fair and just judgments.

> *Reverence for the LORD is good; it will continue forever. The judgments of the LORD are just; they are always fair. Psalms 19:9*

As months of my keeping distance passed, the better behavior from others remained and I began to reevaluate my judgments. Was I being fair? I hadn't completely found the answers I was looking for when I made the decision to withdraw, but the initial pain I felt had time to subside and become a bit more bearable.

Making fair judgments wasn't as easy a concept as I thought it should be. I didn't look at the people who were in my life and see them as inherently "bad" people, and there were people who appreciated having me in their life, at least to some degree. Yet, there I sat in the middle of a life that lacked fulfillment.

What causes you to struggle in making fair judgments?

_____

_____

_____

_____

_____

---

28 *Merriam-Webster's Dictionary and Thesaurus,* Updated Edition, s.v. "Just."

How can you show appreciation to someone in your life by valuing them more fairly?

_____

_____

_____

_____

_____

—ɯ—

Lesson 4: Regard

Whether we like it or not, all of us communicate with multiple people almost every day. In the technology-dominated world we live in, email has become one of our primary forms of communicating with others. There is a certain type of structure that goes into writing emails, and part of that structure includes a closing line followed by a signature.

Although the most popular closing line in an email is *Sincerely*, many people close their emails showing some type of "regard" by saying something like *Warmest regards* or *Kindest regards*. We likely aren't thinking about the deeper meaning of showing regard when making those closing remarks, but the Bible demonstrates for us just how important having regard for others is:

People with no regard for others can throw whole cities into turmoil. Those who are wise keep things calm. Proverbs 29:8

One might read that verse and think it has a harsh tone to it. Not showing regard for someone can throw a whole city into *turmoil?* Granted, most of us haven't literally seen a whole city get thrown into turmoil, but what truth resides in that verse? Turmoil doesn't just have to look like a whole city getting taken down. Turmoil also looks like an unhealthy team environment because of not regarding someone's input on an important decision.

In my case, turmoil looked like broken trust in a relationship because of someone else showing zero regard for my boundaries. For a short while, I was under the impression that the turmoil I experienced was starting to dissipate. Little did I know just how wrong I was! The improvement was short-lived, and any hope I gained from it along with any ounce of worth I saw in myself got taken away from me in a matter of seconds the night I was raped.

Within an instant, that Proverbs verse became my entire life. *I* was that whole city that was thrown into turmoil. How could anyone have *such little regard* for someone else that they force sex on someone who said they had no interest in doing so? To this day, I can't give a good answer to that question, because there isn't one. No *means* no!

As much as I would've liked to, I couldn't take away what happened to me. I was furious, and I took my anger straight to God, crying "What just happened, and what did I do to deserve this?" The disrespect that person showed penetrated straight to my soul. I wasn't even sure I could respect *myself* anymore. I had just been taken advantage of. My body felt used and disgusting, and nothing in my power could change it.

Think of a time when someone disregarded you. What was the result?

_____

_____

_____

_____

Think of a time when you disregarded someone else. What was the result?

_____

_____

_____

_____

_____

The verse in Proverbs states that we are to show regard to "others," but who is included in that statement? The book of Psalms gives us a more descriptive answer:

Blessed are those who have regard for the weak; the LORD delivers them in times of trouble. Psalms 41:1 NIV

At that point in my life I had no concept of how God saw me. I also had no interest in pursuing a relationship with God, but he began a new work in me the night I was raped. One could say I subconsciously knew the truth behind Psalms 41:1 even though I hadn't picked up my Bible in years. If there was one thing I knew that night, it was that what happened to me wasn't fair. I didn't ask for it. Yet, there I sat. Defeated. This wasn't how things were supposed to be. I wanted out! I was weak, and I needed *deliverance.*

David declares in the first half of that verse that when we have regard for the weak, we will be *blessed.* The question is, who or what is considered weak?

"Watch and pray so that you will not fall into temptation. The spirit is willing, but the flesh is weak." Matthew 26:41 NIV

Every single one of us has fallen to temptation at some point. In other words, we are to have regard for *everyone*. David then goes on to say that when we have regard for the weak, God will deliver us from times of trouble. What does this deliverance look like?

> *For we do not have a high priest who is unable to sympathize with our weaknesses, but one who in every respect has been tempted as we are, yet without sin. Hebrews 4:15 ESV*
> *. . . but God shows his love for us in that while we were still sinners, Christ died for us. Romans 5:8 ESV*

We can see here just how strong Jesus is—and he the source of our deliverance. Jesus, subject to the same temptations as described in Matthew, lived a life free from sin by not giving in to the weakness of the flesh. After living that life free of sin, he died to pay for our sins. As a result, he *delivered* us from the punishment we all deserve.

How would I find this deliverance for myself? The answer remained a mystery. Something I knew with clarity however was that the way I related to both myself and those around me would never be the same. One could say I had hit "rock bottom" —and as weak as I felt, any rock in my way was too heavy for me to move.

How can you watch and pray that you will not fall into temptation?

_____

_____

_____

_____

_____

How has God delivered you during times of weakness?

_____

_____

_____

_____

_____

How can you empathize with the weaknesses of those around you?

_____

_____

_____

_____

_____

—m—

Dear God,

I acknowledge that in order to show respect to someone in the forms of love and fairness, I must first see their value as you see their value and not in the way the world sees their value. Give me the strength to refrain from anger and boasting, and to instead put my hope in you. I admire how you made me and everyone on this earth both fearfully and wonderfully. Everything you create is wonderful and deserves to be treated with admiration and respect. I confess that I don't always fully appreciate the opportunities or the people that you have placed in my life, and I ask for your forgiveness for those times where I have judged someone unfairly as a result. Thank you for being a God who sets an example by always judging fairly and who appreciates me enough to be willing to pay the death I owe for my sinful nature. Jesus was tempted in every way I am tempted, yet he conquered those temptations by living a sinless life, and then he died for the sins of all so that my sin may be judged in his death rather than my own. Thank you for being the perfect example of respect for me to always turn to.

In Jesus' name,

Amen.

Chapter Seven

THEY ARE WORTHY

Lesson 1: Value

Everything on this earth holds worth, but how much? That depends on who we ask. The determination of worth is a decision we all make on a daily basis, and no two of us make that decision in the same way.

If we were to walk up to a chemist and ask, "What are the precious metals?" the answer would include gold, silver, platinum, and palladium. These metals earn the title of *precious* by being valuable. Their presence is rare, and as a result, they hold a high level of worth.

What do you think gives something worth?

_____

_____

_____

Have you ever invested in something only to later question whether your investment was worth it? What caused you to have those feelings?

_____

_____

_____

_____

Worthy: *adjective* having worth or value; marked by personal qualities warranting honor, respect, or esteem[29]

Any action we take—or don't take, for that matter—is the result determining the worth of something. With every purchase we make, we declare that the product we purchased was worth the amount we invested in it. When we attend an event, we declare that both the event we attend and the people performing in it are worth a certain amount of our time. Our perception of how to determine worth changes multiple times over the course of our lives in response to the changes of our life's circumstances.

Being raped was one of those circumstances in my own life. The way I determined worth, starting with my own worth, would never be the same after that night. My boundaries—violated. My body—tainted. My worth—diminished.

I knew that I didn't ask for what happened to me, but the world didn't give me much reinforcement on that front. I was open about what happened early on, and I was often faced with questions like "What did you say?" and "What were you wearing?" These kinds of responses did nothing but further reinforce my feelings of a diminished worth.

To say that those responses left me shocked would be an understatement. Those responses communicated to me that I wasn't fully believed. Anyone

---

29 *Merriam-Webster's Dictionary and Thesaurus,* Updated Edition, s.v. "Worthy."

else who has been there knows how not feeling believed after going through a traumatic experience further solidifies feelings of worthlessness.

As a result, I began to isolate myself more. I wanted no part of my life to remind me of that night, and I wanted no part of being around people who helped those destructive thoughts rule my mind.

How have you struggled to see your own worth?

_____

_____

_____

_____

_____

The more easily we see the value in any person, product, or experience, the more likely we are to invest in it. If we are guaranteed to get back more value than we put into our investment, economics tells us to take that investment every single time.

This very principle rules each of our actions on a day-to-day basis. Our human nature constantly talks to us and says to invest in what brings *us* the most value. The problem is, our sinful human nature doesn't determine value in the same ways that God determines value. How does God determine value?

> "Look at the birds of the air: they neither sow nor reap nor gather into barns, and yet your heavenly Father feeds them. Are you not of more value than they?" Matthew 6:26 ESV
>
> "Are not two sparrows sold for a penny? And not one of them will fall to the ground apart from your Father. But even the hairs of your head are all numbered. Fear not, therefore; you are of more value than many sparrows." Matthew 10:29–31 ESV

He went on from there and entered their synagogue. And a man was there with a withered hand. And they asked him, "Is it lawful to heal on the Sabbath?"—so that they might accuse him. He said to them, "Which one of you who has a sheep, if it falls into a pit on the Sabbath, will not take hold of it and lift it out? Of how much more value is a man than a sheep! So it is lawful to do good on the Sabbath." Then he said to the man, "Stretch out your hand." And the man stretched it out, and it was restored, healthy like the other. Matthew 12:9–13 ESV

What is the common denominator that Jesus speaks of in each of these passages in which he states what is valuable?

_____

_____

_____

_____

_____

God sees each one of us as valuable as the people Jesus spoke to in those passages. If we are going to see people in the same way as God sees them, we need to see their value in a similar way. Better yet, we should look for opportunities to actively communicate to those around us the value they possess. If there's anything the enemy really enjoys telling us, it's that we are worthless. That couldn't be further from the truth, because God values everyone!

Even though anything telling us we are worthless is lying, being worthless was what I believed about myself in my new season of life, and Satan did a great job of keeping it my truth. My all-time low self-worth made it a cinch to continue drinking. If I stayed in my mind, all I could think about was that night. I needed out!

My problem was that I saw no way out. Instead, I drank my thoughts out of my mind. Drinking didn't give me a refreshing sense of worth, but it did help me forget my lack of a sense of worth. Forgetting my lack of self-worth made drinking helpful enough for me to continue doing it. Where was this path going to lead me though? To this day, I couldn't really say. What I *do* know now is that it would take someone seeing my value in the same way Jesus spoke of value in the passages from Matthew for me to realize I had a bigger purpose.

How have other people communicated the value that both they and God see in you?

_____

_____

_____

_____

_____

How have you communicated to others the value that both you and God see in them?

_____

_____

_____

_____

_____

Lesson 2: Warrant

What is the first thing that comes to mind when you hear the word *warrant*? My guess is for most, you thought about a warrant issued by the police. Police who want to issue a warrant need evidence that the object of the warrant (person or place) is worth searching.

When looking at the definition for *worthy*—"marked by personal qualities warranting honor, respect, or esteem"[30]—we see another use for the word *warrant*. This take on the word *warrant* isn't as commonly used in language, but it is crucial for us to understand what it means in order to fully grasp the worth of the people around us. Unlike police-issued warrants that are issued to investigate a crime of some kind, we see from the definition of *worthy* that the cause warranting our worth is our personal qualities. That leads us to an important question: Would God, the Creator of all mankind, give only certain people qualities deserving of worth?

> *Then Peter began to speak: "I now realize how true it is that God does not show favoritism but accepts from every nation the one who fears him and does what is right." Acts 10:34–35 NIV*

He would not give some people qualities more deserving of worth than others. God does *not* play favorites. He gave us all every quality we possess. If our qualities weren't worth having, he wouldn't have given them to us in the first place! God also doesn't give others certain qualities and then not give them to us because he loves them more. He loves us all the same—unconditionally!

Unfortunately, the world we live in plays the game of favoritism, *a lot*. Racism, sexism, ageism, and many other types of discrimination all stem from the world communicating favoritism to specific groups of people. This favoritism then gives off the message to the people who are on the wrong side of the favoritism that they don't have as much worth.

---

30 *Merriam-Webster's Dictionary and Thesaurus,* Updated Edition, s.v. "Worthy."

What about those on the right side of the favoritism? They get privilege. The world says their personal qualities have a worth that warrants that privilege. Often, they didn't even ask for their privilege; the world just handed it to them.

How has your view of your worth been affected because of someone showing favoritism to someone else over you?

_____

_____

_____

_____

How can you take a step toward showing less favoritism to those around you?

_____

_____

_____

_____

With my low sense of self-worth, I didn't feel my personal qualities warranted much good. I lived each day feeling used, disgusted, and hopeless. I didn't feel like I deserved friendships with anyone that I saw as having a "higher" worth than I saw in myself, and I didn't feel like I deserved any future relationship with a "good" man.

My lack of self-worth also began to affect other areas of my life, starting with school. My grades plummeted; I received my lowest GPA in a semester ever. I didn't land an internship as expected for the program I was in, and I began to wonder what I was doing there in the first place.

Fortunately for us, even though our own view of what our qualities warrant can change over time, God's view of us remains constant. What do our personal qualities warrant in the eyes of God? To answer this, consider this well-known verse:

> *For God so loved the world that he gave his one and only Son, that whoever believes in him shall not perish but have eternal life. John 3:16 NIV*

The word I want us to focus on in that verse is *whoever*. The message of Christ setting us free from our sins is for *everyone*. There is no combination of personal qualities that God's love doesn't cover. In God's eyes, each and every person on this planet was worth the cost of his one and only Son's life.

What qualities of your personality do you feel make you unworthy of love?

_____

_____

_____

_____

Is there anyone you've had a hard time showing love to because of certain qualities they possess? How can you ask God to show you the love he has for that person?

_____

_____

_____

_____

The concept illustrated in John 3:16 was one I had little understanding of in that season of my life. I saw myself being very costly to love, and it affected the way I saw those around me. I didn't know how to overcome that cost to love myself, and I didn't expect anyone else to know either.

A few months later, a new semester of classes began. These new classes opened a door to bring in new people into my life. I soon found myself sitting in the back of a classroom, talking with the girl sitting next to me. I had little expectation of gaining a friendship in the process, but I was soon proven wrong. After a couple of weeks of class, even after seeing all the hurt I carried with me everywhere I went, she didn't change the way she interacted with me. I didn't know how she had that ability, but I did know that she clearly saw something in my qualities that I didn't. That friend wasn't the only one who saw good qualities in me; God did, too.

God sees qualities in every single one of us that we don't see for ourselves. Out of love, he created each of us in his image and marked us with a specific set of qualities. When we embrace the fullness of God's love for us, we can walk—and even run—with confidence along the path that God marks out for us.

Therefore, since we are surrounded by such a great cloud of witnesses, let us throw off everything that hinders and the sin that so easily entangles. And let us run with perseverance the race marked out for us, fixing our eyes on Jesus, the pioneer and perfecter of faith. For the joy set before him he endured the cross, scorning its shame, and sat down at the right hand of the throne of God. Consider him who endured such opposition from sinners, so that you will not grow weary and lose heart. Hebrews 12:1–3 NIV

Without even knowing it, the race marked out for my life took a sharp turn toward finding the *joy* spoken of in those verses. In order to find that joy, I had to let go of the sin that entangled my life. The problem was, I wasn't ready to let go yet. Although it was nice to make new friends, the hurt in my heart remained, and I continued my life of drinking. The bottle was too good a friend for me to abandon it that soon.

What path has God marked for you, and what sin is entangling you from being able to run on that path with perseverance?

_____

_____

_____

_____

_____

—m—

Lesson 3: Honor

You've been invited to an award ceremony in which a project you worked on received "honorable mention." Depending on how much effort you put into the project, you may be disappointed with that result. But the truth is, the reason you were even given the honorable mention accolade is because the judges saw your project as *worth* mentioning. Although this is just one type of showing honor, any time honor is shown, it is done in recognition of worth.

For us to be people who recognize the worth in others, we must know how to show honor. Showing honor is a paramount characteristic in God's desire for the type of people he wants us to be. In fact, it's so important to him that he includes honor in the Ten Commandments.

"Honor your father and your mother, that your days may be long in the land that the LORD your God is giving you." Exodus 20:12 ESV

This doesn't mean we get a pass from showing honor those who aren't our parents. We see the concept of showing honor appear in a broader context in the New Testament:

Love must be sincere. Hate what is evil; cling to what is good. Be devoted to one another in love. Honor one another above yourselves. Romans 12:9–10 NIV

How has someone else honored you above themselves? Did their actions help you see your worth?

_____

_____

_____

_____

_____

How can you show honor to someone in your life to communicate the worth you see in them?

_____

_____

_____

_____

_____

My new friend became a tangible example in my own life of showing honor to one another when she invited me to attend church with her. She knew about the darkness surrounding my life. She also knew I hadn't stepped foot in a church environment in years, and it didn't stop her from asking me. I felt honored that she thought to include me and I went with her that week.

Notice how my friend didn't learn about my issues and then *tell* me I needed to go to church—she *asked* me to go with her. God operates in this same mindset. He would never tell us to do something that he wouldn't also do. Just as God calls us to be people who show honor, God shows honor to us.

> *"Whoever serves me must follow me; and where I am, my servant also will be. My Father will honor the one who serves me." John 12:26 NIV*

How, then, can we be people who intentionally show honor? Qualities associated with honor are:

Kindness: *Whoever pursues righteousness and kindness will find life, righteousness, and honor. Proverbs 21:21 ESV*
Generosity: *Whoever oppresses a poor man insults his Maker, but he who is generous to the needy honors him. Proverbs 14:31 ESV*
Grace: *A gracious woman gets honor, and violent men get riches. Proverbs 11:16 ESV*

A few days later, I found myself at the church service my friend invited me to. I quickly found out that with Thanksgiving on the horizon, the entire service would be dedicated to people sharing what they were thankful for. Feeling bold, I made my way to the stage and shared my thankfulness. Thankfulness that someone invited me there. Thankfulness for a new beginning.

Following the service, I made my way to the campus library in the building next door. Before I knew it, people who had been at the same service walked past me and began introducing themselves. They told me they were glad that I came and that I shared. After five or six of these introductions, I knew it was more than just a coincidence. I couldn't believe so many people wanted to make the effort to get to know me!

Everyone who came and talked to me that night emulated the characteristics of showing honor. They were kind in making the initiative to speak to me and generous in inviting me to join them again. They honored the fact that I showed up, and it blew my mind. Making the decision to return the following week was a no-brainer.

When was a time in your life where showing kindness, generosity, or grace resulted in honor?

_____

_____

_____

_____

_____

How can you show more kindness, generosity, or grace in a situation you're currently going through?

_____

_____

_____

_____

_____

Jesus also displayed the qualities of kindness, generosity, and grace perfectly through his death on the cross.

But because of his great love for us, God, who is rich in mercy, made us alive with Christ even when we were dead in transgressions—it is by grace you have been saved. And God raised us up with Christ and seated us with him in the heavenly realms in Christ Jesus, in order that in the coming ages he might show the incomparable riches of his grace, expressed in his kindness to us in Christ Jesus. Ephesians 2:4–7 NIV

By his sacrifice, Jesus honored us and took on the payment we all deserve to bear. He did this as an expression of kindness, so that we might experience the riches of being made alive by his grace.

How has receiving God's grace made you more alive?

_____

_____

_____

_____

_____

—⟋⟍—

Lesson 4: Lasting Worth

In the market for buying a new car, you make your way to a dealership. Upon your arrival, a car salesman approaches us and offers us two cars for the same price. They are the same make and model, but one of them is brand new and the other is ten years old. Which one do you buy? Obviously, the newer one—but why? Over time and repeated use, cars lose their value—they aren't *worth* as much.

This phenomenon of changing value is common among the material objects of this world—even money. Anyone in business will tell you that a dollar today is worth more than a dollar ten years from now.

When we focus on only the material things of this world, this concept of worth makes perfect sense. Dependent on factors such as time, labor, materials, and product usefulness, the value of material goods varies. However, if we begin to implement this same philosophy of determining worth to define both our self-worth and the worth of others, problems arise. Unlike the products in this world made from the work of humans, people are the creation of God. We are *his* workmanship.

For we are his workmanship, created in Christ Jesus for good works, which God prepared beforehand, that we should walk in them. Ephesians 2:10 ESV

How does knowing that God has prepared good works for you change your view of your own lasting worth?

_____

_____

_____

_____

_____

Notice how Paul, the author of Ephesians, specifically says that not only are we God's workmanship, but that he also prepared our works beforehand. What exactly does that mean? To me, it means two things. First, it means we don't get to be the ones who determine our own worth or anyone else's worth. God made us, and he is the *only* one who gets to determine our worth. Second, it means our worth isn't determined by how well we perform.

This concept behind determining worth was a new one for me. In the partying world, worth primarily resulted from performance—materially, competitively, and physically. If I wanted to gain worth at a party, a few simple steps of bringing the best alcohol, drinking the most drinks, and making out with some guy were sure to bring positive results. But those things weren't lasting; they were good for only one night. If I wanted to find worth again, I had to go back for more. I had to buy the alcohol again, drink the drinks again, and make out with the guy again. The problem with doing all that? It's unhealthy and not how God created us to operate.

Shortly after exploring the church environment again, my body began to reject my efforts for satisfying my craving for worth. I physically couldn't drink like I used to anymore; my body refused. I went from being able to keep up with everyone drink for drink to not being able to stomach even one beer. What was I going to do?

The logical answer to that question would be to just quit drinking, but that was a lot easier said than done. Why? Because quitting entails a lot more than "just quitting." Quitting required me to give up something that had been providing worth in my life. At that time, removing the worth my lifestyle provided for me was far more painful than throwing up the alcohol I could no longer handle the next morning.

In what ways have you allowed your works to determine your worth?

_____

_____

_____

_____

_____

How has your perception of others' worth changed based on their works?

_____

_____

_____

_____

_____

Thankfully for us, our worth to God never changes. As the omniscient Creator of all mankind that God is, he isn't surprised by any of our actions. God knew full well that we would all fall to sin, and that doesn't change how much he loves us.

> *But God has shown us how much he loves us—it was while we were still sinners that Christ died for us! Romans 5:8*

It was God's plan from the very beginning to send Jesus to die for the sins of all. What does this mean? Not only can we experience eternal life with God, but we can also know we have been and always will be worthy enough to receive Jesus's payment for our sins. Jesus's death on the cross will *always* be enough to forgive our sins.

I love how that verse demonstrates for us that God did not wait for us to stop sinning before he sent his Son to die for us. Why? Because that day would have never come! As long as we inhabit this earth separated from God, we will sin; our human nature can't help it.

I'm going to guess I'm not alone in this, but I can tell you that if God was a God who waited for me to be perfect, that's not a God I want to serve. The good news is, he doesn't wait. Jesus died while we were still sinners because our sin separates us from God, and God doesn't want any of us to live another day separated from him. Any messages we hear that condemn us or diminish our worth are not from God!

Where is condemnation most prevalent in your life?

_____

_____

_____

_____

How does that condemnation affect your view of your worth?

_____

_____

_____

_____

How can you be a light to someone else in your life and show them the lasting worth they have?

_____

_____

_____

_____

—〜—

Dear God,

Thank you for being a good Father, and thank you that my worth to you never changes—I confess that I don't see those around me with as much value as you do. Provide me with an opportunity to show someone in my life how valuable they are. I pray against anything that prevents me from walking with confidence on the path you laid for me. Thank you for being a God who constantly extends grace and kindness to me, even in the times where I wandered off that path. Help me to see that, at the end of the day, your view of my worth is the only view that matters, so that I can be free to extend that same grace and kindness to others. It is by that same grace that you saw me as worthy enough to die for, and anything telling me I'm not worth that price tag is not from you. I am grateful that my worth to you will never diminish, and I ask that you give me the ability to treat others with the same mindset.

In Jesus' name,

Amen.

Chapter Eight

THEY ARE GOD'S IMAGE

Lesson 1: Likeness

Images surround us everywhere we look. These images can range from pictures we take and upload to our social media page, to the image we portray in our everyday words and actions. We have the access to consume more images on a daily basis than ever before, and the pressure from society to be a certain image increases accordingly. How do we choose which one to portray?

For the first time in years, I had to seriously ask myself this question. The answer was no longer cut-and-dried. In the time leading up to my stepping into a church environment again, my life revolved around living up to a certain image. That fact alone made it that much harder to quit drinking. I found myself in the middle of a lose-lose battle. If I stayed in my current lifestyle, I lost by failing to live up to the image I built for myself.

If I left my current lifestyle, I would lose everything on which I had built my image.

Leaving my lifestyle seemed like the best option, but I wasn't willing to fully dive-in. I couldn't take the risk of leaving and losing my community as a result. Because of my fear, I pursued both paths of life for a while. One day I went to a party with one group of friends, and the next day I went to church with a different group of friends.

I knew that the pain of isolation was more than I could handle. Although my fear of losing my community didn't come from a good place, truth does reside in how God didn't create us to live in isolation. Community was in his design of creation from the very beginning with Adam and Eve.

Have you had the experience of needing to live up to a certain image? If so, how did that affect your life?

_____

_____

_____

_____

_____

Image: *noun* a likeness or imitation of a person or thing; a picture of an object formed by a device (as a mirror or lens); a vivid representation or description[31]

We see images utilized frequently during the process of creation. Many man-made creations are born out of having a physical or mental image of something and bringing that image to reality. The process of God creating mankind also involved the use of an image—*God's* image.

---

31 *Merriam-Webster's Dictionary and Thesaurus,* Updated Edition, s.v. "Image."

So God created mankind in his own image, in the image of God he created them; male and female he created them. Genesis 1:27 NIV

What does it mean to you that God made you in his image?

_____

_____

_____

_____

_____

Looking to the first definition, we see the word *likeness,* or in other words, *resemblance* and *similarity.*[32]

In our case, the "person or thing" we were made in the likeness of is God. Because of that, we all resemble God in some way. Backing up one verse in Genesis, we see God confirm how we are made in his likeness.

Then God said, "Let us make mankind in our image, in our likeness, so that they may rule over the fish in the sea and the birds in the sky, over the livestock and all the wild animals, and over all the creatures that move along the ground." Genesis 1:26 NIV

The distorted image I saw of myself and my view of my self-worth fueled much of my fear of leaving my old lifestyle. Don't get me wrong, making new friends was an extreme blessing, and it reassured me to know people didn't see me the way I saw myself. However, simply having the knowledge that they didn't see me in the same way wasn't enough to change my own view of myself.

The voices in my head were too strong. "Your body is tainted." "You don't have the worth you once did; it was taken from you." "You don't

---

32 *Merriam-Webster's Dictionary and Thesaurus,* Updated Edition, s.v. "Image."

deserve a good future relationship; no one will want you." I didn't know how to mute the taunting, but I was willing to step out of my comfort zone and do what it took to find an answer.

Soon after I began exploring church again, my friend invited me to join her in the Bible study small group in her dorm. Doing this provided an opportunity to discover on a deeper level what it meant to be made in God's likeness. Part of resembling God and being made in his likeness is being made for community. Community is key to God's design down to the fact that he is triune in nature as Father, Son, and Holy Spirit. Participating in the group also allowed me to get to know other women's stories to a greater degree and provided hope in knowing I could bring lasting change in my own life.

How do you resemble God?

_____

_____

_____

_____

How do you see a resemblance of God in those around you?

_____

_____

_____

_____

Being made in God's likeness doesn't just stop at his creation of us. When we receive the Spirit of God, we become transformed into his likeness.

But it can be removed, as the scripture says about Moses: "His veil was removed when he turned to the Lord." Now, "the Lord" in this passage is the Spirit; and where the Spirit of the Lord is present, there is freedom. All of us, then, reflect the glory of the Lord with uncovered faces; and that same glory, coming from the Lord, who is the Spirit, transforms us into his likeness in an ever greater degree of glory. 2 Corinthians 3:16–18

Freedom lives anywhere the Spirit of God is present. Anyone who invites in and possesses the Spirit of God can access that freedom at all times and in all places. Sounds great, right? The problem is, most of us live completely unaware of the greatness of that freedom.

I can say with confidence that I received the Holy Spirit on that night in middle school when I prayed to God to take my nightmares away, but I still remained clueless to the power and freedom found in God's Spirit. Regardless of not knowing this freedom on a personal level, I felt freedom in the small groups I began attending. The people around me knew this freedom and I was determined to find it.

If something truly transforms us, how can we *not* want to share that with those around us? To be genuinely transformed and then not share with others how to find that same transformation is the ultimate level of selfishness and is completely outside of God's nature.

How has your life been transformed by freedom?

_____

_____

_____

_____

_____

How can you share that transformation with others?

_____

_____

_____

_____

_____

—ɯ—

Lesson 2: Imitation

Imitation is a skill we all possess naturally. Anyone who has been around a toddler for more than a few minutes knows how toddlers constantly imitate the words and actions of those around them. Toddlers share a strong desire to both learn from and be like their parents and other influential people in their lives. In other words, as the definition "a likeness or imitation of a person or thing"[33] suggests, they portray an image of those they imitate.

A key difference between toddlers and adults is the fact that toddlers will imitate just about anything. Toddlers do not possess the level of discernment needed to determine if what they imitate is good or bad. That's why adults become more sensitive about their words and actions around toddlers to prevent them from imitating bad behavior. Just as we want to caution a toddler's imitation of bad behavior, John gives us a similar instruction:

My dear friend, do not imitate what is bad, but imitate what is good. Whoever does good belongs to God; whoever does what is bad has not seen God. 3 John 1:11

---

33 _Merriam-Webster's Dictionary and Thesaurus,_ Updated Edition, s.v. "Image."

The toddler analogy applies to more than just people who are two or three years old. Similar in nature to how we all have a physical birth, anyone who receives the Holy Spirit is said to be "born again" with the Spirit.

Jesus answered, "Very truly I tell you, no one can enter the kingdom of God unless they are born of water and the Spirit. Flesh gives birth to flesh, but the Spirit gives birth to spirit. You should not be surprised at my saying, 'You must be born again.' The wind blows wherever it pleases. You hear its sound, but you cannot tell where it comes from or where it is going. So it is with everyone born of the Spirit." John 3:5–8 NIV

In this time of joining a small group for the first time, I was very much in a "toddler" stage of Christianity. I didn't know what it looked like to live my life for God, but I now had people around me who did. I began to get more involved quickly as the opportunities to get more involved arose.

Aside from attending church and the Bible study regularly, one of those first opportunities involved going to a conference over New Year's Eve. This opportunity proved to be quite the contrast from the New Year's Eve prior. Instead of spending the night getting too drunk to recall most of what happened, I stood among thousands of other Christian college students as we collectively prayed over the year to come.

On both of those nights, I had people who looked out for me. The ways they "looked out for me" manifested itself very differently. On the night that involved getting drunk, the care looked like making sure I didn't pass out or hurt myself if I fell. On the night that involved praying in the New Year, the care looked like a joy-filled room of people allowing me to come alongside them. They made sure I had the experience of belonging, and they prayed with me for the year to come.

Being someone who was new to the faith-based way of life, I felt awkward praying in general, let alone out loud and around that many people. If I'm honest, I still find praying awkward at times, but that doesn't change the importance of prayer. Anything preventing us from praying to God is *not from God!*

What does "imitating what is good" mean to you?

_____

_____

_____

_____

_____

In what ways do you see a difference in the images you portray to others when you imitate something good versus something bad?

_____

_____

_____

_____

_____

We all know that doing good is the right thing to do, but it isn't always the easy thing to do. God tells us how there will be some suffering involved in doing what is good. In those hard times, we can remind ourselves of the benefits from doing good.

When we do what is good, we:

Glorify God: *"In the same way, let your light shine before others, so that they may see your good works and give glory to your Father who is in heaven." Matthew 5:16 ESV*

Please God: *Do not neglect to do good and to share what you have, for such sacrifices are pleasing to God. Hebrews 13:16 ESV*

Reap Harvests: *So let us not become tired of doing good; for if we do not give up, the time will come when we will reap the harvest. Galatians 6:9*

The presence and absence of these three qualities by imitating good versus imitating bad came as expected in both of my New Year's Eve experiences. Nothing about getting excessively drunk glorifies or pleases God—it merely makes a fool of the one getting drunk and then reaps the harvest of a hangover for the majority of the next day. On the other hand, God experiences the utmost pleasure when we come to him in prayer. Our prayers and God's provision from those prayers allows us to reap harvests beyond our human capacity. When provision happens in ways that only God can make happen, it brings glory to him and the world can't help but notice!

How have you seen the benefits of glorifying God, pleasing God, or reaped a harvest from doing good in your own life?

_____

_____

_____

How have you become tired doing good for others, and how can God give you the strength to not give up?

_____

_____

_____

It is important to point out that although God calls us to do good, there is a huge difference between doing good as a response to God's goodness and doing good in an effort to gain salvation. Salvation comes through faith alone, not through works!

> *". . . know that a person is not justified by the works of the law, but by faith in Jesus Christ. So we, too, have put our faith in Christ Jesus that we may be justified by faith in Christ and not by the works of the law, because by the works of the law no one will be justified. But if, in seeking to be justified in Christ, we Jews find ourselves also among the sinners, doesn't that mean that Christ promotes sin? Absolutely not!"* Galatians 2:16–17 NIV

Paul makes an important distinction here, saying how even though we aren't saved by our works, it doesn't give us the permission to sin as we please. In our sinful human nature, the concept of not promoting sin is a lot easier said than done. The ease of us getting stuck in our sin cycles makes it crucial for us to encourage one another to do good along the way. But how do we become people who imitate good?

Paul mentions this same concept of imitation in his letter to the Ephesians:

> *Therefore be imitators of God, as beloved children. And walk in love, as Christ loved us and gave himself up for us, a fragrant offering and sacrifice to God.* Ephesians 5:1–2 ESV

If we want to be imitators of good, we need look no further than imitating God. God is good all the time. He uses all parts of our stories for good, and he would never ask us to imitate him if he didn't have our best interest in mind.

How can you better apply being an imitator of God in an area of your life?

_____

_____

_____

_____

_____

How can you encourage those around you to be in a community of people who do good?

_____

_____

_____

_____

_____

—ɱ—

Lesson 3: Picture

At some point in life, we've all been in a situation that seemed *unbelievable* in some way. If we told a friend about the situation and they didn't believe us, they would likely ask us if we had a "picture" to prove it. What happens if we don't have a picture? The chances of them believing us would likely be slimmer, but why? Pictures provide evidence of something's existence and act as a source of proof.

The pictures we take vary in color, shape, and size, but each picture produces its own unique image. Taking the definition "a picture of an object formed by a device (mirror or lens)"[34] into the context of us capturing an image, the "device" most of us use today is a cell phone. However, when talking about being made in God's image, the "device" forming our image is God.

> *For you formed my inward parts; you knitted me together in my mother's womb. I praise you, for I am fearfully and wonderfully made. Wonderful are your works; my soul knows it very well. My frame was not hidden from you, when I was being made in secret, intricately woven in the depths of the earth. Your eyes saw my unformed substance; in your book were written, every one of them, the days that were formed for me, when as yet there were none of them. How precious to me are your thoughts, O God! How vast is the sum of them! Psalms 139:13–17 ESV*

Does knowing how God intricately and wonderfully made you affect the way you see the image he gave you? Why or why not?

_____

_____

_____

_____

Do you find God's thoughts precious? Why or why not?

_____

_____

_____

_____

---

34 *Merriam-Webster's Dictionary and Thesaurus,* Updated Edition, s.v. "Image."

God made a plan for every one of our lives before we were even born. He created each of us in the exact image of him needed to execute that plan. How do we get to a place where we believe that, though? The truth is, if we don't see our own image in the same way he sees it, we won't understand God's plan for our life.

What exactly do I mean by that? I mean that if we don't see our image through the same lens that God sees us, we are incapable of seeing ourselves as fit for the purpose for which God made us. What does this incapability of seeing look like in actuality?

I struggled for years to see my body's worth in the same way God saw my worth. Even after getting involved with church again, my struggle remained. How did I struggle to see my worth? For me, it was less about my external body image and more about my internal body image. Going on a diet or hitting the gym were never going to cure my skewed perception. I needed a transformation of my *mind*, not a transformation of my physique. My thoughts of myself were not the same as God's thoughts of me. How do I know that? It's simple. My thoughts of myself were everything *but* precious.

Now I know how part of what God has for the rest of my life on earth is to be a light to other survivors of sexual assault—to be an example of hope and to show them they have worth. During my first couple of years of going back to church, I had no idea I could be a positive light to other survivors. How could I be that kind of light for other survivors if I couldn't see any hope or worth in myself? I couldn't.

In what area do you struggle to see your image in the way God sees your image? How does that impact the way you see those around you?

_____

_____

_____

Just as God had a plan for us, God had a plan for bringing Jesus to this earth—a plan to reconcile us back to him through the death of his one and only Son. God isn't surprised by our sin or the price we owe for committing a sin. God wants a relationship with us. His interest in having that relationship is so high, he will do whatever it takes to achieve it—even if it means having Jesus die in our place.

> *Long ago, at many times and in many ways, God spoke to our fathers by the prophets, but in these last days he has spoken to us by his Son, whom he appointed the heir of all things, through whom also he created the world. He is the radiance of the glory of God and the exact imprint of his nature, and he upholds the universe by the word of his power. After making purification for sins, he sat down at the right hand of the Majesty on high, Hebrews 1:1–3 ESV*

We all know our physical looks portray an image, but our looks aren't the only image we portray; our actions portray an image of us as well. The author of the passage above tells us that if we want a picture of how God works, look no further than to Jesus, who shares in God's exact nature. In sharing God's nature perfectly, Jesus portrayed an image unlike any other human to walk this earth.

After Jesus died on the cross, he imparted to us the Spirit of God, which allows *us* to share in God's nature. On our own, we are powerless. With God's Spirit, we possess his power and the capability to live in the image we were truly made for!

In what ways do your actions resemble the nature of God?

_____

_____

_____

How could you improve on resembling God's nature to those around you?

_____

_____

_____

_____

—m—

Lesson 4: Vivid

If someone needing glasses stood in front of a beautiful landscape and looked at it both with and without their corrective lenses, they would see two different images. Did the landscape itself change? Of course not! But just because the landscape stayed the same, that doesn't invalidate the fact that the person still saw two vastly different images. Wearing glasses allowed the person to see the scenery more *vividly*.

This concept of vividness is seen in the definition of *image*, which is "a vivid representation or description."[35] When it comes to images, how the image is formed or portrayed tells only one side of the story. Another side we need to take into consideration is how we perceive the image. Anytime we misperceive an image, we miss out on part of the essence of that image.

> **Vivid:** *adjective* producing a strong impression on the senses; producing distinct mental pictures[36]

Each of us portrays a very distinct—vivid—image of God that no other human created will ever possess. The distinctness of the image each

---

35 *Merriam-Webster's Dictionary and Thesaurus,* Updated Edition, s.v. "Image."
36 *Merriam-Webster's Dictionary and Thesaurus,* Updated Edition, s.v. "Vivid."

of us were created as is not up for our questioning! The problem with us recognizing our vividness is that many of us struggle or have struggled with clearly perceiving our own distinctness.

What is something that has prevented you from seeing your own distinctness, and how did that affect you?

_____

_____

_____

_____

_____

My inability to perceive my own distinctness remained as long as I viewed my body's worth as insignificant. It took me more than a year of going to church consistently before God's light hit me to my core with this verse:

> *Do you not know that your bodies are temples of the Holy Spirit, who is in you, whom you have received from God? You are not your own; you were bought at a price. Therefore honor God with your bodies. 1 Corinthians 6:19–20 NIV*

These verses spoke directly to my biggest struggle—seeing my body, my *image* in the way God saw me. God saw me with a greater degree of vividness than I saw myself. To him, my body wasn't worthless. Quite the contrary—my body was worthy enough to him to be a temple of his Spirit. I saw my body as more like a broken-down shack, maybe a studio apartment at best. But a temple? No way! But my view of myself didn't stop God from seeing my worth.

What's the significance of Paul declaring that we are temples of the Holy Spirit? In the Old Testament, God's presence resided in a temple, in a place called the Holy of Holies. The Holy of Holies was covered by a veil, and only the high priest could enter the Holy of Holies after a sacrifice of an unblemished animal took place.

When Jesus, the Lamb of God, died on the cross, he fulfilled the sacrifice needed. Jesus's death on the cross tore the veil to the Holy of Holies, and when we receive his sacrifice, *we* become the temples where God's Spirit resides. Crazy, right? To us, it might sound crazy, but to a God and Father who desires nothing more than to be in community with us, it's not crazy at all.

What are you currently struggling to see in your life, and how can you ask God to help bring you clarity?

_____

_____

_____

_____

I strongly desired to know how God viewed me in such a way, and I became more willing to do what it took to find that clarity for myself. I can't say I gained the clarity I wanted overnight. It took me another year of going to church and taking in God's word before I really felt like my body held that kind of value. Even then, finding my value didn't come through some "magical" experience one day. Instead, I found my value by becoming more familiar with God's truth over time, and in doing so, experiencing clarity when facing lies from the enemy.

Taking into consideration how God made every human in his image, we need to also be aware of the clarity with which we view others. Since no two people in the world share the exact same image of God, each one of our images serves a unique purpose. Jesus calls us to not be people who judge one another—which includes judging their images.

> *"Do not judge others, so that God will not judge you, for God will judge you in the same way you judge others, and he will apply to you the same rules you apply to others. Why, then, do you look at the speck in your brother's eye and pay no attention to the log in your own eye? How dare you say to your brother, 'Please, let me take that speck out of your eye,' when you have a log in your own eye? You hypocrite! First take the log out of your own eye, and then you will be able to see clearly to take the speck out of your brother's eye." Matthew 7:1–5*

This passage touches on how we like to point out things that prevent others from seeing clearly before we first address what prevents us from seeing *them* clearly. If we don't remove the log from our own eye first, we will never be able to fully see the images of those around us.

When have you tried addressing the speck in someone else's eye without first addressing the log in your own? What was the result?

_____

_____

_____

_____

_____

How does this concept of vividness come into play when looking at being made in God's image? A similar analogy to the viewing of the landscape can be applied in the context of how we view God. The nature of God never changes!

Jesus Christ is the same yesterday, today, and forever. Hebrews 13:8

Even though God himself doesn't change in nature, our *view* of God almost certainly changes over the course of our lives. When we learn more about God and grow our faith in him, we gain a more vivid, or clearer, image of God.

How has your view of God changed over time? What enabled you to view him differently or with greater clarity?

_____

_____

_____

_____

_____

How has your view of others changed as a result of a change in how you view God?

_____

_____

_____

_____

_____

Dear God,

Show me in a new way how you created me to resemble you. You created me and everyone else around me in your image, and there is no bad image of you. Please continue to transform me into your likeness with your glory, and use me as a vessel to continue bringing your glory to this earth. I confess that I don't always want to do good—especially when life gets hard—but I desire to live my life in a way that is more pleasing and glorifying to you. Thank you for being a God who doesn't wait for me to become a good person to earn salvation. Your goodness speaks for itself, and your thoughts about me are always precious. I ask for you to replace my thoughts about others with your precious thoughts about them. Give me your eyes to see everyone as the beautiful and unique image you created them in, and not as the distorted image the world tells them they should be. Your goodness will never change, and neither will my value as being an image-bearer of you.

In Jesus' name,

Amen.

Chapter Nine

THEY ARE FRIENDS

Lesson 1: Attachment

As I finalized the topics for this book, I looked at the list of twelve topics and wondered exactly how this chapter fit in with the rest of the book. After much thought, I kept it because I couldn't get this passage out of my mind:

> *"My command is this: Love each other as I have loved you. Greater love has no one than this: to lay down one's life for one's friends."*
> *John 15:12–13 NIV*

In this passage, Jesus states how there is no greater love than to lay down our lives for our *friends*. What makes that declaration so important? The very crux of Christianity stands on the fact that Jesus Christ laid down his life on the cross for our sins. There is no one on this earth for whom

Jesus didn't willingly sacrifice his life. What does that mean? If Jesus wasn't *willing* to be friends with everyone, he wouldn't lay down his life as a payment for the sins of *everyone*.

What does laying down your life for your friends mean to you?

_____

_____

_____

_____

_____

It is important to note that even though Jesus invites us all to accept his sacrifice, it's up to us to accept his invitation. Jesus already made the investment on his end to become our friend, and when we accept his investment, that friendship is confirmed.

Do you see Jesus as your friend? Why or why not?

_____

_____

_____

_____

_____

Before we get too far into this chapter, I want to address the topic of enemies. Enemies exist. Saying that enemies don't exist would be far from the truth—even God himself has enemies. Who are God's enemies?

But God has shown us how much he loves us—it was while we were still sinners that Christ died for us! By his blood we are now put right with God; how much more, then, will we be saved by him from God's anger! We were God's enemies, but he made us his friends through the death of his Son. Now that we are God's friends, how much more will we be saved by Christ's life! Romans 5:8–10

Every single one of us has been God's enemy at some point. It was while we were still enemies with God that he sent Jesus to die for us—to reconcile us back to him. Being enemies with God didn't stop him from loving us, and God calls us to be that same type of person. To be a friend of God's looks like showing love to all, even to our enemies.

"You have heard that it was said, 'Love your friends, hate your enemies.' But now I tell you: love your enemies and pray for those who persecute you, so that you may become the children of your Father in heaven. For he makes his sun to shine on bad and good people alike, and gives rain to those who do good and to those who do evil." Matthew 5:43–45

What can you do to be a person who more intentionally loves your enemies?

_____

_____

_____

_____

_____

What I do hope for everyone is that this chapter will shift our viewpoint both in the ways we approach our current friendships and in how we view forming new friendships. Jesus didn't place any preconceived judgments on our looks or personality traits when deciding to lay down his life for us, and we shouldn't look down on others for those reasons either!

What exactly does being a friend to someone look like?

Friend: *noun* one attached to another by respect or affection; one who is not hostile; one who supports or favors something[37]

For this first lesson, we will focus on attachment. When we are close friends with someone, others might describe our friendship as people being, "*attached* at the hip." In the context of both that phrase and the definition of *friend*, the word *attach* means, "to join in action or function; make part of."[38]

What functions have you joined or are a part of? Do you see yourself as friends with others who are involved in those same functions? Why or why not?

_____

_____

_____

_____

_____

Joining a church again gave me a set of friends I always wanted but never knew I needed. For the first time in my life, I had women investing in my life in a mentorship capacity. Women who gave up their time each week to meet with me. Women who believed I was more than I thought. Women who helped me discover my value in Christ. They joined me on my walk with God, just as everyone who calls Jesus a friend is joined together.

---

37 *Merriam-Webster's Dictionary and Thesaurus,* Updated Edition, s.v. "Friend."
38 *Dictionary.com,* s.v. "Attach," accessed June 28, 2020, https://www.dictionary.com/

So then you are no longer strangers and aliens, but you are fellow citizens with the saints and members of the household of God, built on the foundation of the apostles and prophets, Christ Jesus himself being the cornerstone, in whom the whole structure, being joined together, grows into a holy temple in the Lord. In him you also are being built together into a dwelling place for God by the Spirit. Ephesians 2:19–22 ESV

Typically, when we think of being attached to something, we associated high value to it and don't want to be separated from it. God associates that same level of value to everyone he creates. As a result of our value to him, he sent his Son so that we never again have to be separated from him because of our sin.

No, in all these things we have complete victory through him who loved us! For I am certain that nothing can separate us from his love: neither death nor life, neither angels nor other heavenly rulers or powers, neither the present nor the future, neither the world above nor the world below—there is nothing in all creation that will ever be able to separate us from the love of God which is ours through Christ Jesus our Lord. Romans 8:37–39

The goodness of God resides in the fact that he never lets anything stop him from showing love to us. How different would our world today look if we operated with the same mindset? My guess is it would be unrecognizable in a good way. With the power of God's Spirit, we have the power to play a part in bringing that kind of heaven-like culture to earth.

What have you allowed to separate you from loving those around you?

_____

_____

_____

_____

_____

—🙷—

Lesson 2: Affection

When it comes to being a friend to someone, having a sense of attachment tells only part of the story. We must also be aware of *how* that attachment manifests itself. In the first part of the definition of *friend*, the two forms of attachment described are those of respect and affection.

Since we dig deeper into the concept of respecting others in another chapter, we're now going to explore what showing affection looks like. In thinking about how and where we display affection, I most commonly see it in the form of communicating a romantic love for another person. We see people around us daily who are with people for whom they have romantic affection. If we feel like they've gone too far in showing their romantic affection, we call that a "public display of affection" (PDA). But are the people we find romantic interest in the only people we should show affection to? What else can showing affection look like?

> **Affection:** *noun* a feeling of liking and caring for someone or something: tender attachment[39]

---

[39] *Merriam-Webster.com,* s.v. "Affection," accessed June 28, 2020, https://www.merriam-webster.com/

If I'm honest with myself, I often find the concept of affection to be awkward. I care deeply for the people in my life, but I regularly feel like I miss the mark in actually showing it. One could say I am much more of a "thinker" than a "feeler" when it comes to processing which actions to take.

Does that mean I'm bad at showing affection though? Not necessarily. I possess the feelings of caring for others just as the definition for *affection* states, but my mind just tells me I'm bad at showing it. Why? Because I think showing affection should look a certain way and then I don't live up to my own expectations.

Notice how the definition for *affection* doesn't insinuate that our affection for someone manifests itself only in a physical or sexual manner. Just as there are multiple ways to express love, there are also many ways to express affection. Having multiple ways to show affection doesn't make showing it any easier, though—showing affection to those around us can be hard.

How do we make it a point to communicate to those around us that we care for them? Although the way we show our care varies from person to person, the "why" behind showing that care should look the same.

For us to show affection and care for others like God does, we must show our care by not expecting any gain on our end. Jesus cares about each one of us enough to sacrifice his entire life for us, and he did so solely for *our* gain. Jesus didn't need to die so *he* could be in community with God; he died so that *we* could be in community with God.

Caring for our friends and not expecting any gain from doing so on our end goes completely outside of our human nature. If we relied on our own power and ability to properly care for those around us, we would find ourselves eventually coming up short. To make up for our coming up short, God himself graciously grants us with the power to show affection.

His divine power has granted to us all things that pertain to life and godliness, through the knowledge of him who called us to his own glory and excellence, by which he has granted to us his precious and very great promises, so that through them you may become partakers of the divine nature, having escaped from the corruption that is in the world because of sinful desire. For this very reason, make every effort to supplement your faith with virtue, and virtue with knowledge, and knowledge with self-control, and self-control with steadfastness, and steadfastness with godliness, and godliness with brotherly affection, and brotherly affection with love. 2 Peter 1:3–7 ESV

In this passage, we see that love is the supplement to affection. What does love being the supplement to affection mean?

Supplement: *noun* something added to complete a thing, supply a deficiency, or reinforce or extend a whole[40]

If love is the supplement to affection as Peter describes, we can conclude that without love, affection is *incomplete.*

Joining a church community and women's groups supplied a deficiency in my craving for connection. Those people were an example of God's care for me; they took time out of their schedule to meet with and invest in me every week while expecting nothing in return. Learning more about how much God and those around me cared for me allowed me to learn how to care for, love, and see value in myself. By learning how to better love myself, I gained a greater ability to extend love and affection to those around me.

Knowing the benefits that came from gaining friendship and a sense of community among a group of women planted a seed in my heart to be that same kind of person for other women. I was nowhere near the Bible scholar many of my friends were, but my heart for service led me to join a group who planned women's ministry events.

---

40   *Dictionary.com,* s.v. "Supplement," accessed June 28, 2020, https://www.dictionary.com/

I don't mention my—at that time—new-found heart for women's ministry to make myself sound like some incredible and Spirit-led child of God. I'm mentioning it because prior to that point in my life, I would have been *incapable* of joining such a group. Why? Not because I was incapable of physically attending, but because before that time I didn't carry the kind of affection needed to be God's light to other women. My love for God finally started to become real enough to invest back into his kingdom.

Is it possible to show affection to someone without first having love for that person? Why or why not?

_____

_____

_____

_____

_____

When was a time you showed affection to someone and how did it make them feel?

_____

_____

_____

_____

_____

We can't be people who show affection to those around us unless we possess love for them first—more specifically, possess *God's* love for them. Our human nature is selfish. If showing affection involves feelings of caring for someone other than ourselves, then it requires us to act outside our human nature.

What effect does displaying affection to one another have on our lives? Continuing on in Second Peter, we see a picture of the outcomes of living a life both with and without the qualities of love, brotherly affection, godliness, steadfastness, self-control, knowledge, virtue, and faith.

> *For if these qualities are yours and are increasing, they keep you from being ineffective or unfruitful in the knowledge of our Lord Jesus Christ. For whoever lacks these qualities is so nearsighted that he is blind, having forgotten that he was cleansed from his former sins. Therefore, brothers, be all the more diligent to make your calling and election sure, for if you practice these qualities you will never fall. For in this way there will be richly provided for you an entrance into the eternal kingdom of our Lord and Savior Jesus Christ. 2 Peter 1:8–11 ESV*

Living a life absent of those qualities comes as a product of forgetting how Christ displayed each of those qualities to us. Forgetting how Jesus died on the cross and cleansed us from our sins causes us to be nearsighted to the point of blindness.

In contrast, living a life that embraces those qualities enables us to walk our path with confidence. God promises us that we will not fall. Not only will we stand victorious, but we will also be richly provided for by gaining eternal life with Christ, and it doesn't get any better than that!

How has your lack of showing affection come as a result of forgetting what Christ has done for you on the cross?

_____

_____

_____

How has your success in showing affection allowed you to walk more confidently?

_____

_____

_____

_____

How can you extend affection to someone in your life right now?

_____

_____

_____

_____

—∿—

Lesson 3: Hostility

Hostility is a topic that influences our news headlines every day. Whether it's something as large as political hostility that effects a whole nation, or as small as a child refusing to let another child play with their toy, our world today has no issue making sure its hostility gets heard. Why is that? What exactly are we trying to accomplish when we express hostility? One thing is for certain: when we express hostility, we aren't expressing it with the intention of becoming *friends* with those people.

To see others in a "friend" context, we need to rid our lives of hostility; as the definition states, a friend is "one who is not hostile."[41] How do we know if the way we relate to those around us creates hostility?

---

41 *Merriam-Webster's Dictionary and Thesaurus,* Updated Edition, s.v. "Friend."

Hostile: *adjective* of, relating to, or characteristic of an enemy[42]

When we show hostility toward people regardless of whether it's our intention, what we're essentially doing is relating to them as if they are our enemies. Having a hostile mentality toward the people around us couldn't make Satan any happier! Why? Because nobody on this earth is an enemy we should be concerned about fighting against—*he* is. If we see those around us as our enemy, it distracts us from having awareness for Satan and his evil schemes. God warns us of those schemes and instructs us to put on his armor to fight against them.

Put on all the armor that God gives you, so that you will be able to stand up against the Devil's evil tricks. For we are not fighting against human beings but against the wicked spiritual forces in the heavenly world, the rulers, authorities, and cosmic powers of this dark age. So put on God's armor now! Then when the evil day comes, you will be able to resist the enemy's attacks; and after fighting to the end, you will still hold your ground. Ephesians 6:11–13

Where does hostility exist in your life currently?

_____

_____

_____

_____

_____

---

42   *Dictionary.com,* s.v. "Hostile," accessed June 28, 2020, https://www.dictionary.com/

How can you put on the armor of God to help you fight against your hostility?

_____

_____

_____

_____

_____

The ultimate enemy of our world is Satan. What does that mean for us? If Satan is the enemy, and hostility shows up when we exemplify characteristics of an enemy, then we can expect hostility to show up in this world any time Satan is involved. If we know how Satan moves, then we can live intentionally in not creating hostility by simply not replicating those same behaviors.

"The thief comes only in order to steal, kill, and destroy. I have come in order that you might have life—life in all its fullness. I am the good shepherd, who is willing to die for the sheep." John 10:10–11

What characteristics does Satan possess? Satan does everything with the intention of stealing, killing, or destroying. To have the mentality of someone who sees others as a friend—rather than an enemy—we must do the opposite of what Satan does; we need to be people who give, help, and build rather than steal, kill, and destroy. Giving, helping, and building, are all qualities present in God's nature, and God encourages each of us to live in the same way:

<u>Give:</u> *"Do not judge others, and God will not judge you; do not condemn others, and God will not condemn you; forgive others, and God will forgive you. Give to others, and God will give to you. Indeed,*

you will receive a full measure, a generous helping, poured into your hands—all that you can hold. The measure you use for others is the one that God will use for you." Luke 6:37–38

Help: *Help carry one another's burdens, and in this way you will obey the law of Christ. If you think you are something when you really are nothing, you are only deceiving yourself. You should each judge your own conduct. If it is good, then you can be proud of what you yourself have done, without having to compare it with what someone else has done. For each of you have to carry your own load. Galatians 6:2–5*

Build: *For God did not appoint us to suffer wrath but to receive salvation through our Lord Jesus Christ. He died for us so that, whether we are awake or asleep, we may live together with him. Therefore encourage one another and build each other up, just as in fact you are doing. 1 Thessalonians 5:9–11 NIV*

After about a year of being involved in building friendships through women's ministry, I came to a point where I had some important decisions to make. My time left until graduation grew short, and the need to figure out life's next steps became a top priority. I didn't know where I wanted to go, but I did know that I wanted to move out of the state and explore graduate school in a different city. I prayed for God to open an opportunity to make that move possible and he answered my prayer with an acceptance to attend graduate school 1,600 miles away.

This answer to my prayer came a number of months in advance of having to move. Knowing that I was preparing to leave everything I had built up over the past few years, I made the conscious effort to reflect on all the blessings my friends were to me during that time by writing to them. I wrote many letters—not only to thank them for how they gave to me and helped build me up, but also to build them up in return.

For someone whose first love isn't writing, writing all those letters could have been daunting. Thankfully, it was far from daunting—and if I'm honest it was fun and somewhat freeing. Why? For the first time in my life, I invited God in to guide me on my path. He answered my prayer, and I felt good about where my life was heading. The purpose and clarity I felt in my path freed me to focus on the "now" and to intentionally love those God had placed in my life while I still had time.

Satan could do nothing to steal, kill, or destroy my mission and hostility had no place of welcome. I carried the armor of God and committed myself to giving back the love my friends poured into me. By writing those letters to give to and build up those around me, it created a space for them to see how I viewed and related to them as a friend.

In what ways has someone given to, helped, or built you up in some way? What is your relationship to that person?

_____

_____

_____

_____

_____

How can you give to, help, or build up someone in your life who is in need of a friend?

_____

_____

_____

_____

Lesson 4: Support

Everyone on earth was born for a specific purpose. No matter how different our purposes are, we all work together to create one beautiful story written by God. Deep down, we all want a supportive culture—it is the very essence of how God created us. None of us was created to execute our purpose alone.

Anyone who puts their faith in Jesus belongs to the *body* of Christ. Just like all the parts of our physical bodies connect with and support the other parts, anyone who belongs to the body of Christ is there by design to support other people. But God's design of us supporting one another wasn't a new concept that arrived when Jesus came into the picture. God made it known as soon as he created mankind that our purpose is for more than just us.

> *The LORD God said, "It is not good for the man to be alone. I will make a helper suitable for him." Genesis 2:18 NIV*

By creating Eve, God provided Adam with a helper, or supporter, because it was not good for Adam to be alone. Leaning on the fact that God's word is true, living, and active, we can apply this same principle to our own lives—it is not good for us to be alone, either. Knowing how God made us to support those around us means nothing unless we put it into practice. Being "one who supports or favors something"[43] is in the very nature of what it means to be a friend. How do we be that friend to others and show those around us that we are there to support them?

---

43 *Merriam-Webster's Dictionary and Thesaurus,* Updated Edition, s.v. "Friend."

When was a time you *did* feel supported by someone? What did they do and why did that make you feel supported?

_____

_____

_____

_____

When was a time you *did not* feel supported by someone? What did they do (or fail to do) and why did that make you feel unsupported?

_____

_____

_____

_____

__Support:__ *verb* to maintain (a person, family, establishment, institution, etc.) by supplying with things necessary to existence; provide for[44]

Supporting one another comes as a product of two things—provision and supplication. Provision and supplication aren't things we would do for someone we saw as our enemy. However, I think it's safe to say that all of us would provide or support someone we saw as a true friend. Many of us find it uncomfortable to ask for provision and supplication when we need it—including me. Satan likes us to think that needing provision or supplication of some kind is a sign of weakness. The truth is, needing provision or supplication just means we need a *friend.*

---

44 *Dictionary.com,* s.v. "Support," accessed June 28, 2020, https://www.dictionary.com/

Showing our need for provision is far from a sign of weakness; we all need provision on a regular basis. There's no shortage of opportunity in our world to provide for those around us. Jesus also speaks on this topic and says that there will always be poor people in our world.

> *"You will always have poor people with you, but you will not always have me." Matthew 26:11*

When Jesus says in this verse that we will not always have him, he speaks in a physical sense, foreshadowing to his death on the cross. By his death, Jesus left us with the Holy Spirit so we could then be God's vessels of provision on this earth. The problem is, part of our human nature needs to know we have been provided for first. After all, how can we provide for someone without having anything to provide? We can't. Even though we can't rely on our own strength to provide for those around us, we *can* rely on God. God stops at nothing to provide us with our every need.

> *"So do not start worrying: 'Where will my food come from? or my drink? or my clothes?' (These are the things the pagans are always concerned about.) Your Father in heaven knows that you need all these things. Instead, be concerned above everything else with the Kingdom of God and with what he requires of you, and he will provide you with all these other things. So do not worry about tomorrow; it will have enough worries of its own. There is no need to add to the troubles each day brings." Matthew 6:31–34*

How have you seen God provide for you?

_____

_____

_____

How has God's provision of your needs allowed you to support others?

_____

_____

_____

The good news is, God *promises* provision to us—we don't ever have to question his support. Like we touched on briefly at the beginning of this lesson, living both in support of and providing for one another is the very essence of how God designed the body of Christ.

> *Instead, by speaking the truth in a spirit of love, we must grow up in every way to Christ, who is the head. Under his control all the different parts of the body fit together, and the whole body is held together by every joint with which it is provided. So when each separate part works as it should, the whole body grows and builds itself up through love. Ephesians 4:15–16*

In my last few months before moving for school, I saw these verses lived out to their fullness in my life. I had a community who built me up in love whenever I needed it and they were there to support me in my preparing to move across the country. I felt good about God leading me to make this move, but it was still terrifying. Making this decision sent me back into a very familiar space of moving locations and separating myself from a significant number of friendships.

The last time I made the commitment to move locations in my life, I did so on my own accord and I moved back home to a safety net of past friendships. The last time I purposefully removed myself from friendships, I did so because I was in a season of extreme darkness and I needed to remove myself from my old lifestyle.

This time, the separation looked a little different. I made the commitment to move because I felt God's call to move. This time, I prepared to move away from every friendship I had made in life to date. Unlike removing myself from friendships that were unhealthy, these friendships were extremely life-giving and the pain of leaving them hit a little differently.

Even though I felt good overall about committing to life out west, I couldn't help but think, *What was this all for? Why would God take me out of my flourishing community and send me to a place where I knew no one?* I didn't know the answers to these questions. What I *did* know is that I would have to trust God in ways I never had before if I wanted to succeed. He was going to be the only one making this move with me.

What can you do to build up someone around you in love?

_____

_____

_____

_____

_____

Dear God,

Thank you for wanting to be my friend. Your desire to be my friend is so strong that you sent Jesus to give up his life for mine. Your value for me is so high that you desire to never again be separated from me. By your love you gave us victory, and there is nothing on this world powerful enough to take that victory away from me. Give me the ability to see my enemies in the way you see them, allowing me to look at them through a lens of love rather than hate. I confess that sometimes I forget how much love you have for me. As a result of my forgetfulness, I don't walk with confidence on the path you have laid for me, and I don't always love those you place on my path in the way you desire me to. I acknowledge that the true enemy of this world is Satan and not any of the people in my life. Satan comes only to bring hostility, and he attempts to steal, kill, and destroy any good thing you have for me. You call me to be a person who gives to, helps, and builds up those around me, and I ask that you will put someone on my heart that I can be that light to. Thank you for always being there to support me, and for giving me the assurance and knowledge that I will always be taken care of.

In Jesus' name,

Amen.

Chapter Ten

THEY ARE DEARLY LOVED

Lesson 1: Precious

Are we loved? It's a question that isn't often verbalized, but is one we seek to answer daily. All of us are born with the desire to be loved—to know we are cared for.

Showing love is of utmost importance to God—so much so, that when the Pharisees tested Jesus on what the greatest commandment is, Jesus centered his answer to them around love:

> *"Teacher, which is the greatest commandment in the Law?" Jesus replied: "Love the Lord your God with all your heart and with all your soul and with all your mind.' This is the first and greatest commandment. And the second is like it: 'Love your neighbor as yourself.' All the Law and the Prophets hang on these two commandments." Matthew 22:36–40 NIV*

Why do you think Jesus included the second most important commandment of "love your neighbor as yourself" in his answer when the Pharisees asked him for only the *greatest* commandment?

_____

_____

_____

_____

_____

I'm not saying anything new when I say we all want to be loved for who we are, so I'm not going to spend time trying to convince anyone on *why* we should love others. Instead, I want us to dig deep into *how* we should love—or, rather, how *God* loves. In the following passage, Paul describes God's love as "dear."

Follow God's example, therefore, as dearly loved children and walk in the way of love, just as Christ loved us and gave himself up for us as a fragrant offering and sacrifice to God. Ephesians 5:1–2 NIV

What do you think it means for someone to be dear to you and for you to love them accordingly?

_____

_____

_____

_____

_____

Dear: *adjective* highly valued: precious; high in price: expensive[45]

---

45   *Merriam-Webster's Dictionary and Thesaurus*, Updated Edition, s.v. "Dear."

Before any of us begin to doubt for a second and think that we are not dear to God, look no further than to the first two words of the definition for *dear*—highly valued. God values each one of us enough to give us his Son as an offering and sacrifice for the sins we committed. No one else will ever value us as much as God values us. Because of our high value to God, his love for us is precious.

> *How precious is your steadfast love, O God! The children of mankind take refuge in the shadow of your wings. Psalms 36:7 ESV*

The best part about the precious nature of God's love is that it's steadfast. That means, his love for us and the value he sees in us never changes! We have always been dear to God, and the same goes for everyone else in our lives.

Who is someone you find precious and why?

_____

_____

_____

_____

_____

Out of the nature of God's love, he sent Jesus down to earth to shed his precious blood for our sins.

> *For you know that it was not with perishable things such as silver or gold that you were redeemed from the empty way of life handed down to you from your ancestors, but with the precious blood of Christ, a lamb without blemish or defect. He was chosen before the creation of the world, but was revealed in these last times for your sake. Through him*

you believe in God, who raised him from the dead and glorified him, and so your faith and hope are in God. Now that you have purified yourselves by obeying the truth so that you have sincere love for each other, love one another deeply, from the heart. 1 Peter 1:18–22 NIV

Through faith, each one of us has the option to accept the payment Jesus offered to us. Once we place our faith in him, the debt we owe to sin becomes purified and wiped clean. To God, our faith in him is more precious than gold.

Be glad about this, even though it may now be necessary for you to be sad for a while because of the many kinds of trials you suffer. Their purpose is to prove that your faith is genuine. Even gold, which can be destroyed, is tested by fire; and so your faith, which is much more precious than gold, must also be tested, so that it may endure. Then you will receive praise and glory and honor on the Day when Jesus Christ is revealed. 1 Peter 1:6–7

Moving across the country for graduate school was a trial unlike any I had encountered before. Like the trials described by Peter in the verses above, this trial came with its fair share of sadness and suffering. I moved a few weeks before classes started, and moving into an environment where I had no established friendships made for a lot of loneliness. I didn't even know any of my classmates before stepping foot on campus for our first day of class.

Going from a community I loved to one where I knew virtually no one within a five-hundred-mile radius tested my faith in a way that forced me to rely on God more than I ever before felt I needed to. Like every trial's purpose, God used this trial to prove whether my faith was genuine. This test of faith included only one question—if God was the only person I had, would he be enough?

I'd like to tell you that my answer from the start was *yes*, but it wasn't that easy. What I can tell you is that my new environment made for many new opportunities to love those around me dearly. By having God's Spirit, I carried every tool necessary to capitalize on those opportunities. When we place our faith in God and receive his Spirit, it allows us to love one another dearly—or, as Peter describes it, deeply, sincerely, and from the heart.

How has God recently tested your faith?

_____

_____

_____

_____

How has someone else loved you deeply, sincerely, or from the heart?

_____

_____

_____

_____

How can you show love to someone else in your life in a manner that is deep, sincere, and from the heart?

_____

_____

_____

_____

—◁◁◁—

Lesson 2: Expensive

Everything that exists in our world has some level of value attached to it. The amount of time, skill, and materials put into a product helps determine its price. The level of value an item has to us is largely subjective to our own personal interests, but the way we treat items based on our perception of their value remains constant. The more expensive an item is to us, the more *dearly* we treat and care for it. We can apply this same concept when it comes to the way we treat the people around us. The more we see the value in another person, the more dearly we treat them.

Reading that last sentence may give the impression that I'm saying that some people are more valuable than others, but that couldn't be further from the truth. In the eyes of God, no one person is more valuable than another. The amount to which God dearly loves us does *not* change from person to person! God loves unconditionally.

What prevents you from seeing the same level of value in everyone?

_____

_____

_____

_____

_____

Unlike God's love, our human love comes with conditions. If we are to love others as God loves, we must change our mindset. What does that difference in mindset look like? We see this difference illustrated well in the story of the woman and the alabaster jar:

Jesus was in Bethany at the house of Simon, a man who had suffered from a dreaded skin disease. While Jesus was eating, a woman came in with an alabaster jar full of a very expensive perfume made of pure nard. She broke the jar and poured the perfume on Jesus' head. Some of the people there became angry and said to one another, "What was the use of wasting the perfume? It could have been sold for more than three hundred silver coins and the money given to the poor!" And they criticized her harshly. Mark 14:3–5

In this first part of the passage, we see the mindset of man. Here we have a woman who pours an extremely expensive jar of perfume—which she likely loves very much—on Jesus' head. The reaction of those around her as she pours the perfume was a reaction filled with anger, judgment, and criticism.

How are anger, judgment, or criticism present in your life right now?

_____

_____

_____

_____

What is the cause behind that anger, judgment, or criticism?

_____

_____

_____

_____

The people there couldn't believe that she acted so boldly with something of such high value. They disapproved of her actions so much that they told her she *wasted* the perfume by pouring it onto Jesus's head! As if that wasn't harsh enough, they then pointed out how much of a waste they thought her actions were by saying how much she could have sold the perfume for.

In their interaction, we see a classic example of what Jesus speaks of in the Sermon on the Mount when he says: *"You cannot be a slave of two masters; you will hate one and love the other; you will be loyal to one and despise the other. You cannot serve both God and money."* *Matthew 6:24*

The people watching this interaction despised the woman's actions. They served money, but the woman served Jesus. It could be easy for us to read that passage and think about how harshly they treated the woman, but the truth is, none of us are any better than them. If we forget about who Jesus really is and what he's done for us, giving up all we have for him will look like a waste to us too, every single time!

Looking at the situation of God asking me to surrender my community to him could have also easily looked like a waste. Why would he ask me to give up something so valuable to go to a place where I had to start from ground zero? Talk about an *expensive* investment!

Clearly, God didn't think my investment to move was a waste, or he wouldn't have led me to do it to begin with. How then, can we look at the same situation from God's viewpoint? Continuing in the passage, we see how Jesus responds to their despise after the woman poured the perfume on him:

> But Jesus said, *"Leave her alone! Why are you bothering her? She has done a fine and beautiful thing for me. You will always have poor people with you, and any time you want to, you can help them. But you*

will not always have me. She did what she could; she poured perfume on my body to prepare it ahead of time for burial. Now, I assure you that wherever the gospel is preached all over the world, what she has done will be told in memory of her." Mark 14:6–9

When the woman poured the perfume on Jesus, what the others saw as a "waste" Jesus saw as a "fine and beautiful thing." Trying to appear thoughtful, the others followed up their criticism of calling her act a waste by saying that she could have instead given to the poor—but Jesus had a rebuttal for that too.

Jesus *did not* condemn the thought of giving to the poor. Quite the opposite: he encouraged and welcomed them to give to the poor at any time. What Jesus *did* do was acknowledge the fact that this woman did all she could in giving what she had to him. That bottle of perfume was expensive, and it was *still worth it* to her to pour it onto Jesus—talk about dearly loving someone!

This same concept rings true in our own lives. When I gave up my all to answer God's call in moving, God saw it as a fine and beautiful thing, not a waste! Does that mean God saw a different value in the community I left than I did? Of course not! The value of the bottle of the perfume wasn't what changed in the story of the woman and the alabaster jar—the crowd, the woman, and Jesus all knew the perfume's value. What changed was the perception of Jesus's value. The others saw Jesus's value as "less than" the perfume, and the woman saw his value as "more than." As a result, she treated Jesus more dearly than they did.

In the same way, we must be mindful of the level of value we see in others. Everyone on this earth was expensive enough to die for in God's eyes, and that value never changes for anyone!

What is something in your life right now that has been "too expensive" to surrender to Jesus?

_____

_____

_____

_____

_____

How can you be an encouragement to those around you to help them surrender their all to Jesus?

_____

_____

_____

_____

—⟋⟍—

Lesson 3: Heartfelt

Love is one of the biggest mysteries that exists in this world. We all have our own understanding of love, and we crave being loved daily. We all have a lot to learn about what it truly means to love—saying that we fully understand love is like saying we fully understand God. God *is* love.

Whoever does not love does not know God, for God is love. 1 John 4:8

The mysterious nature of love leaves many of us struggling to find the words to effectively communicate the love we have for those around us. One of the more universal signs used in our world to display love comes in the form of a shape. If we wanted to tell someone around us in a non-verbal manner how we love something, all we'd have to do is draw a heart.

We see reference to hearts in the next aspect of *dear* which simply says "heartfelt."[46] In order to embrace the concept of dearly loving someone, we need to look at what it means to love them in a "heartfelt" manner.

What do you think it means to love someone in a heartfelt manner?

_____

_____

_____

_____

_____

Another way to say "heartfelt" is to use the word *earnest*. When I think of earnest, the first thing that comes to mind is the concept of putting forth an earnest effort—to do as much as possible to accomplish the task at hand. In this case, the task at hand is loving others. Then why is it so important to love one another earnestly?

Above everything, love one another earnestly, because love covers over many sins. 1 Peter 4:8

---

46 *Merriam-Webster's Dictionary and Thesaurus,* Updated Edition, s.v. "Dear."

What prevents you from loving those around you earnestly?

_____

_____

_____

_____

What does Peter mean when he says, "love covers over many sins?" To address this, I want to first cover what that phrase *doesn't* mean. It doesn't mean that it's okay for us to sin whenever we want because love will cover us. God hates sin. Our sin separates us from God—he hates that too. At the end of the day, something that will always be at the top of God's list of desires is for us to have a relationship with him. Sin separates us from God and prevents that relationship from happening without some form of sacrifice being made.

The other thing it doesn't mean is that love "covers over" our sin, "hiding" the sin as though it never happened. God justly punishes all sin.

There are countless people in this world who have been victim to sin and who are hurting badly. The events that happen to them to cause their hurt are very much real, as are the feelings of hurt they experience afterward. Contrary to what Satan wants us to believe, God's love for us doesn't change in the face of sin, and our value to him as a person does not decrease. God will always dearly love us, regardless of our circumstances!

After being raped, *I* was that person who hurt. The feelings of worthlessness and disgust that came as a result were my entire reality at that time. By finding out how much God dearly loved me and by surrounding myself with others who dearly loved me, my life changed forever. The darkness and hurt survivors go through is powerful, and it takes a powerful love to both shine light into and overcome that darkness. God put forth an earnest effort to make sure I knew how dearly he loved me. As a result, he put a deposit in my heart that allows me to show that same heartfelt love to others.

How can you intentionally extend love to someone in your life who is going through a hard time?

_____

_____

_____

_____

_____

Then how *does* love cover sins? Look no further than to Jesus, who set an example of that by dying on the cross.

> *This is love: not that we loved God, but that he loved us and sent his Son as an atoning sacrifice for our sins. 1 John 4:10 NIV*

Jesus covered the sacrifice we all deserve to pay, and he did it because of his dear love for us. What does that mean for us? It means that Jesus paid for our sin so we don't have to. Even though we don't have to re-pay for our sin once we place our faith in Jesus, we all have a lot we can learn and apply in our own lives when it comes to the heart behind Jesus's actions.

Jesus died on the cross in an offering of his life as a sacrifice for ours. He knew full well that God called him to die for us, and he did exactly that without expecting us to pay him back. Our sacrifice for others won't look like dying on a cross for someone else's sin, but we do have other things we can sacrifice—such as our time, money, and other resources—to show our love for those around us.

Moving across the country put me in a place where, for the first time, I began cashing in on those deposits God placed in me for community and women's ministry during the previous years. Instead of people seeking me out, I sacrificed my time to seek out a Godly community. I never wanted to be in another place in life where that kind of community didn't exist in my routine. I knew first-hand the hurt that comes from drifting away from God like I did when I first went to college, and I never wanted to be that far away from the joy found in Christ again. With God's provision, I quickly found a community similar to the one I left behind.

I then looked to use the resources from the women's ministry I was a part of before to start a new women's ministry. By combining my resources with the resources of others God placed on my path, that women's ministry started within a couple of months. Even though "sacrifice" often has a negative connotation, I gained much more than I gave up in this season by giving up my time and resources to get this ministry started. I gained skills that helped me continue to lead the women's ministry, an environment to help me continue to grow spiritually, and an overall feeling of contributing to a greater purpose.

How has someone in your life given up their time, money, or other resources to love you? How did that make you feel?

_____

_____

_____

_____

_____

How have you given up your time, money, or other resources to love someone else? How did it make them feel?

_____

_____

_____

_____

—⁓—

Lesson 4: Special

Imagine you've just been given the news that our house is going to get destroyed by a natural disaster. You have a limited amount of time to grab as many possessions as possible. Which items do you take? The specific items themselves will vary greatly for each person, but one thing that holds true is that all of us would go for the items we find the most *special*.

Considering that *special* is a synonym of the word *dear*,[47] it would stand to reason that the more special something is to us, the dearer it is as well. This concept of being special is a somewhat straight-forward process when it comes to our physical possessions. We know which of our possessions bring us more value than others, because we get to determine whether the value to us is enough for the possession to be called special.

Similarly, how do we see other people in a way that tells them they are special? We need to see the people around us in the same way we see the items we saved from our house that was about to get hit by disaster—we need to see them as being too valuable to destroy. This concept seems simple on paper, but we all know it's not simple at all. Why? Because our world has an enemy who *loves* destroying everything in sight. Destroying is one of his main missions.

---

47 *Merriam-Webster's Dictionary and Thesaurus,* Updated Edition, s.v. "Dear."

The thief comes only to steal and kill and destroy; I have come that they may have life, and have it to the full. John 10:10 NIV

Satan couldn't care less about how special we see our physical possessions. As for the value we see in ourselves and in those around us? He will stop at nothing to destroy our view of them and of ourselves. Why? Because our souls hold infinitely more value than any earthly item ever will. Satan *hates it* when we know how dearly loved we are by God!

Do you see yourself as special? What impact does that have on how you love yourself?

_____

_____

_____

_____

_____

Think of someone who is special to you; how do you love them more dearly as a result?

_____

_____

_____

_____

_____

Unlike with our earthly possessions, we don't possess the authority to determine if someone else is special. Only God himself holds the authority to make that determination. God made each one of us, and he finds us all special in the unique way he created us to be.

The first verses in the Bible describe how God created the universe and all that is in it during the first six days, with the creation of mankind coming on the sixth day. If we look further into God's creation of mankind, we can see how his creation of us was done in a special way.

> *Then God said, "Let us make mankind in our image, in our likeness, so that they may rule over the fish in the sea and the birds in the sky, over the livestock and all the wild animals, and over all the creatures that move along the ground." Genesis 1:26 NIV*

Separate from everything else God created, he created us in his own image. There are billions of different images of God walking on the earth today, and each one of us portrays an image of God that is special and unique to that of any other person.

In addition to the special nature by which we were created, the declaration God made following our creation was also special.

> *God saw all that he had made, and it was very good. And there was evening, and there was morning—the sixth day. Genesis 1:31 NIV*

The key word in that verse is that God saw his creation of us as *very* good. This reaction was special given the fact that in each of the days prior, God stated that what he created was good. Note that mankind didn't do anything special to earn the distinction of being very good versus just good; God simply declared it so.

Our declarations contain power as well. Even though God is the only one who holds the power to speak life into existence from nothing, we do have the ability to speak life into others in the sense of building them up.

Do not let any unwholesome talk come out of your mouths, but only what is helpful for building others up according to their needs, that it may benefit those who listen. Ephesians 4:29 NIV

If someone had asked me where I saw my life heading at the time of starting that women's ministry in my new home, I would've said I had somewhat of a decent idea. God blessed me with opportunities to pursue a great education to set me up for an established career in corporate America. Sure enough, upon graduating with my master's degree, I stepped onto the corporate path and stepped away from leading the women's ministry. Not even a month after starting on this path and thinking I had "made it," I had a rather peculiar conversation.

Without being told any specifics on what it should look like, someone asked me about leading a women's Bible study. They told me to dream up the logistics of this group, including what the group would actually study when it met. On that day, I heard God tell me I already had the message within me for that group, and I needed to start *writing* it. Doubt instantly stirred in my mind, "Are you sure I'm the right person, God? I'm not a writer!" I didn't know what God was thinking.

What I *did* know is that no part of me saw myself as someone qualified to write something like that. I needed a lot of building up from outside sources to make this writing happen. Most of those needs remained unknown to me, but one thing was certain—I needed accountability because if it was left up to me, I'd never put pen to paper.

How has someone else built you up according to your needs?

_____

_____

_____

_____

What are some of the needs of those around you?

_____

_____

_____

How can you speak life into the people around you and build them up according to those needs?

_____

_____

_____

_____

_____

—◠◡◠—

Dear God,

Love is the very essence of who you are. You loved me before I even knew what love was, and you call me to be an extension of your love to those around me. Anything that tells me I am not dear to you is a lie, and I pray against anything attempting to feed those lies to me. The truth is I am so dear to you that you had your Son sacrifice his precious blood for me. After the work on the cross was finished, the price for my sin was paid once and for all. In exchange for that payment, all you ask of me is to have faith, for my faith is so precious to you. I confess that in order to comprehend loving everyone in my life as dearly as you love them, I need a change in mindset. Thank you for being a God whose love is so big and vast that I will never be able to fully comprehend it—and at the same time being a God whose love is in all the details of my life. Give me the ability to love those around me just as they are, so that by being a reflection of you they might get to know how dearly you love them as well.

In Jesus' name,

Amen.

Chapter Eleven

THEY ARE ACCEPTED

Lesson 1: Obligations

The word *accept* wears many different hats in the English language and is used in a wide range of ways. On one end of that range, acceptance comes with a great deal of choice, such as when we receive a job offer and we choose whether to accept it. On the other end, acceptance is largely circumstantial and sometimes out of our control. In those times, we have no choice but to accept our new reality and keep living with the cards we're dealt.

Looking at acceptance in the context of how we see other people in society, we don't have to go very far before we find someone who wants acceptance. We *all* want the comfort of knowing that we have a place where people accept us.

What can you do to create an environment where everyone in your presence feels accepted?

_____

_____

_____

_____

_____

Accept: *verb* to assume an obligation[48]

Acceptance plays a crucial role in our being united with God. Anyone who wants to become a follower of Christ cannot do so before *accepting* his payment for our sins. When we choose to accept Jesus's death on the cross for our sin, we are forgiven of our sin, gifted with the Holy Spirit, and united with God. It is no coincidence that God uses this same method to unite us with him. God is a God of purpose and design, not happenstance. He is a God of love and acceptance, and he calls us to be the same way.

How, then, do we become people who create an environment of acceptance? The definition of *accept* declares that we accept something when we assume an obligation. The question is: Do we have any obligations to assume, and if so, what are they?

> So then, my friends, we have an obligation, but it is not to live as our human nature wants us to. For if you live according to your human nature, you are going to die; but if by the Spirit you put to death your sinful actions, you will live. Romans 8:12–13

What are we obligated to? To not live according to our human nature and to put to death our sinful actions—talk about a bold claim! What

---

48   *Merriam-Webster's Dictionary and Thesaurus,* Updated Edition, s.v. "Accept."

does this obligation mean for us? Our world takes a very weighty and discouraging view on obligations. I'm sure we've all been in a place where we did something only because we felt *obligated* to—in other words, we felt like we *had* to. Viewing obligations in this way leads to apathy or resentment.

On the other hand, God gives us an obligation that leads to *life*. Who doesn't want that? The life God offers is far better than any life we could give ourselves. However, if we're honest with ourselves, we've all been in a place where we didn't want the life God offers. Why? Because putting to death our human nature is hard!

It took me two months after having that moment with God about writing a Bible study before I became willing to sit down and hear more about what he had to say to me. I hadn't *accepted* the life God wanted me to live. My human nature hated books. I wanted nothing to do with them— let alone *write* one! What did I have to say anyway?

Even though I still wasn't fully sure what it would lead to, I decided to put to death my human nature of selfishness long enough to sit down and figure out what the small group study should be about. For the first time, I found myself accepting—or assuming the obligation of—something God specifically placed on my path. It wasn't easy. I had no clue what I had gotten myself into, but I was determined to stick with it. If God is who he says he is, then my acceptance of this calling would lead me to what God had for my future.

What does putting to death your human nature and/or sinful actions look like to you?

_____

_____

_____

_____

Why does Paul, the author of the book of Romans, make a claim as bold as saying we have an obligation to put to death our sinful actions? Earlier on in Romans, Paul writes:

> *For the wages of sin is death, but the gift of God is eternal life in Christ Jesus our Lord. Romans 6:23 NIV*

In other words, the obligation we are required to assume as a result of our sinful actions is death. Not very reassuring, is it? It wouldn't be reassuring if that were the whole story. Thanks be to God, it *isn't* the whole story.

Arguably the greatest news that the Bible has to offer is the fact that Jesus Christ assumed that obligation of death for us. Jesus lived a sinless life. He had *no obligation* to die, yet he did it anyway—for us. Because Jesus died and rose again, no human ever again has to assume the obligation of death as a result of their sins if they accept the obligation Jesus took on for us.

> *For Christ died for sins once and for all, a good man on behalf of sinners, in order to lead you to God. He was put to death physically, but made alive spiritually, and in his spiritual existence he went and preached to the imprisoned spirits. 1 Peter 3:18–19*

Why did Jesus die for us? To lead us back to God. Jesus assumed the obligation of death for *everyone*. God wants to accept every person on this planet into his kingdom. God also wants to make us all alive spiritually. With the power of God's Spirit, we possess the strength and ability to extend acceptance to those around us, even when the world tells us otherwise.

How does it make you feel knowing that God accepts you and has already assumed your obligation of death for you?

_____

_____

_____

_____

_____

Has the fact that God took on the punishment of your sins made you more alive spiritually? If so, how?

_____

_____

_____

_____

_____

How can you further extend the same acceptance that God has for you to those around you?

_____

_____

_____

_____

_____

—ᗡᑎ—

Lesson 2: Care

The message of showing care to those around us is one we all learn how to read at a very early age in life. Regardless of whether a child knows what the word *care* means, all children know whether care is shown to them. If we ignore children or don't take the time to recognize their needs and achievements, we do not leave them with the experience of being cared for.

As with trust, the feeling of acceptance through care[49] can break very quickly and take a long time to restore. What this means for us is that we must be conscious of facilitating a caring environment in our relationships with others right from the *start*—not once we've gotten to know them better.

As much as I try to be a person who cares for those around me in the best way I know how, God has also blessed and surrounded me with caring people. My career as an author would not be what it is today without the care I received from others. After spending a little more than six months getting out of my house at least three nights a week to write, I completed the final lesson of my first book. I then found myself at a standstill and thought, *What now, God?*

I had no idea. God also knew how clueless I was, and a few weeks later he placed someone on my path to provide an answer. Even though we had never met before, after I introduced myself and explained what I was writing about, they instantly told me "You're going to be the next best-selling author." They cared enough about both me and my message from our one interaction to make that become reality and to put me in contact with someone else who could guide me through those next steps.

---

49   *Merriam-Webster's Dictionary and Thesaurus,* Updated Edition, s.v. "Accept."

Who or what are some of the people and things you care about the most and why?

_____

_____

_____

_____

_____

<u>Care:</u> *verb* to feel interest or concern[50]

When we care about something, we have an interest in or concern for it. We are more accepting of it. For the purpose of this lesson, I'm not going to delve into the "right" way to show our care—that looks different for each of us. Rather, I want to focus on what we're putting our care into—more specifically, showing care to other people.

The act of showing care requires us to act differently than our nature tells us to. Our actions toward the things we care both for and about are a direct reflection of the interest and concern we have for it. The Bible is very clear in stating that we should be displaying care to everyone around us in those same ways:

> <u>Interest:</u> *Let each of you look not only to his own interests, but also to the interests of others. Philippians 2:4 ESV*
>
> <u>Concern:</u> *. . . But God has put the body together, giving greater honor to the parts that lacked it, so that there should be no division in the body, but that its parts should have equal concern for each other. If one part suffers, every part suffers with it; if one part is honored, every part rejoices with it. 1 Corinthians 12:24–26 NIV*

---

50 *Merriam-Webster's Dictionary and Thesaurus,* Updated Edition, s.v. "Care."

In what ways do you look to the interests of and show concern for others?

_____

_____

_____

_____

_____

In what ways have others shown an interest in or been concerned for you?

_____

_____

_____

_____

_____

What stops us from showing care to everyone around us? I would argue that the biggest contributor stopping us is our concern with making sure we ourselves are first cared for. We think that if we don't take care of everything ourselves, we will be left in the dust. I'm not saying that if we stop brushing our teeth and making breakfast every morning that someone else will begin to do those things for us. I'm certainly not demeaning self-care, either. Self-care is _extremely_ important.

What I _am_ saying is that we live in a world ruled by fear. I see too many people who hesitate to take steps of faith because worry and anxiety take over. When worry and anxiety begin to control our thoughts, they bring on doubt and cause us to think that if we step into what God is calling us to do, we will for some reason not be taken care of. That couldn't be further from the truth, and that is *exactly* what Satan wants us to believe!

We are called to cast anything causing us to feel the burden of worry and anxiety onto God. No one else can ever care for us or sustain us in the same ways that God cares for us.

> *Cast your burden on the LORD, and he will sustain you; he will never permit the righteous to be moved. Psalms 55:22 ESV*
> *Cast all your anxiety on him because he cares for you. 1 Peter 5:7 NIV*

Those verses don't tell us to cast *some* of our anxiety on him; they tell us to cast *all* our anxiety on him. They also don't say that God *might* sustain us; they say that God *will* sustain us. With that said, why wouldn't we cast our burdens and anxiety on him?

In order to cast our burdens and anxiety onto God, we have to be willing to relinquish our control of them. At times, maintaining control of our burdens and anxiety gives us a false sense of security, when in reality we would be more secure if we just surrendered them to God.

We were not put on this earth to live for ourselves. God gifts us each uniquely with the purpose of using those gifts to benefit others—to care for others.

What anxiety or burden are you currently feeling and how can you cast it over to God?

_____

_____

_____

_____

_____

In what ways has God showed his care for you in the past?

_____

_____

_____

_____

_____

How has God called you to care for others?

_____

_____

_____

_____

_____

—⟋⟍—

Lesson 3: Bear

While we walk through this course called life here on earth, our path brings us into contact with many different people along the way. Whether it's our family, classmates, coworkers, or someone else, many of the people we meet on our path come from sources outside our control. As a result, we've all come across people in our lives whose personalities vary drastically from ours.

The question is, how do we deal with them? If we're honest with ourselves, we all have people in our life we would prefer to not deal with. Sometimes they exhaust us. Other times they just flat out annoy us. In either case, they're in our life for a certain time and it's up to us to decide how we interact with them. If we make the choice to not deal with them, our decision comes with an underlying factor of us saying they are to some degree too much to *bear*.

The word *bear* is used synonymously with the word *accept*.[51] Any time we say someone is too much to bear, we aren't *accepting* them for who they are or where they are in life. By learning how to better bear the differences in those around us, we can be people who lead the way in creating accepting and unifying environments.

Bear: *verb* to accept or allow oneself to be subject to: take on or endure[52]

The Bible uses the word *bear* under a few different conditions. First is the topic of bearing either good or bad fruits. Bearing fruit comes as a product of how we endure our trials on this path called life. The second, and more literal, is the topic of bearing children. For all the mothers out there, I don't think I have to explain why bearing children requires endurance.

In this lesson, I'm going to focus on a third way, which is the concept of bearing burdens. When it comes to accepting people, bearing the burdens of others is essential. The Bible even goes so far as to say that helping others carry their burdens fulfills the law of Christ.

Carry each other's burdens, and in this way you will fulfill the law of Christ. Galatians 6:2 NIV

How has God used you to help carry the burdens of others?

_____

_____

_____

51 *Merriam-Webster's Dictionary and Thesaurus,* Updated Edition, s.v. "Accept."
52 *Merriam-Webster's Dictionary and Thesaurus,* Updated Edition, s.v. "Bear."

How has someone else helped you carry a recent burden of yours?

_____

_____

_____

_____

Let's face it, none of us is promised an easy life. We're only human, and there's only so much our human strength can bear before we reach a breaking point. I'm going to bet almost every single one of us has reached a breaking point—so how do we respond when we reach that breaking point? If we respond to that question with our human nature, the answer would sound something like, "Quit talking to those people" or "Give up."

The burdens leading us to our breaking point can be a combination of both personal burdens and other people's burdens. In either case, if we carry more than we can handle, our ability to accept those around us decreases. God's answer on how to manage the load we carry looks like this:

> _"Come to me, all of you who are tired from carrying heavy loads, and I will give you rest. Take my yoke and put it on you, and learn from me, because I am gentle and humble in spirit; and you will find rest. For the yoke I will give you is easy, and the load I will put on you is light."_ Matthew 11:28–30

Have you ever had the experience of wanting a break from the amount you were carrying? What did you do as a result?

_____

_____

_____

_____

How can you find rest in God by surrendering something you're holding onto?

_____

_____

_____

_____

_____

Soon after being introduced to someone who could help me pursue the next steps of writing my book, I quickly reached a breaking point of my own. The motivation that led me to writing to begin with was the motivation to lead a small group. With that mindset, the original draft of my writing consisted of nothing more than the content for the lessons.

I then got brought to the realization that I needed to include my own story in the lessons too. If I'm honest, I initially didn't think it would be that hard a task. I've shared my testimony verbally more times than I can count. How different could this be?

Turns out, it's a lot different. I wasn't ready for it. I came to a point where I couldn't even *think* about writing my testimony into my book without crying—let alone actually sitting down to write it! I realized then that I put more trust in my ability to say my own testimony than I did in God's ability to use my story for his glory. I placed full responsibility onto myself to carry my burden, to which God said, "Enough is enough." He called me to cast my burden on him so that I could find rest.

Although it is true that we can find rest in God—and that we don't need to carry our burdens on our own—nothing in the Bible suggests that life on earth is free of burdens. Quite the opposite: The Bible actually *guarantees* trials of many kinds and says we are to pick up our cross daily.

And he said to them all, "If you want to come with me, you must forget yourself, take up your cross every day, and follow me. For if you want to save your own life, you will lose it, but if you lose your life for my sake, you will save it." Luke 9:23–24

If we know that we're going to face trials on this earth, what allows us to bear, or endure, them?

Love bears all things, believes all things, hopes all things, endures all things. 1 Corinthians 13:7 ESV

Love allows us to bear or endure our burdens. God loves us way too much to present us with a trial in which his love for us won't help us through! In the same way, we are to extend that same love to others.

Has the simple fact of knowing that you're loved ever helped you endure a trial? If so, in what way?

_____

_____

_____

_____

_____

—⫘—

Lesson 4: Shoulder

We've all been at a point in life where our circumstances felt like they were too much for us to handle. Those feelings could come from personal reasons, such as being overworked at our job. They could also come from communal reasons, such as losing a loved one and gaining a lot of new responsibilities.

When life presents us with the daily challenges of this world, our bodies take on stress. One of the most common places our body places our stress is in our shoulders. Our shoulders are capable of carrying substantial amounts of weight relative to other parts of the body, both metaphorically and physically. In fact, they're so good at carrying weight, terms such as "shouldering the pain" get used in our communication.

Regardless of the cause of the weight, in order for our shoulders to be able to carry that weight or stress, they have to be able to *accept* the physical weight or stress.

What are you currently shouldering?

_____

_____

_____

_____

_____

What circumstances led you to having to carry that weight?

_____

_____

_____

_____

_____

What does this concept of shouldering look like from a spiritual aspect? To answer this, we will look to one of the more well-known parables Jesus taught:

Now the tax collectors and sinners were all gathering around to hear Jesus. But the Pharisees and the teachers of the law muttered, "This man welcomes sinners and eats with them." Then Jesus told them this parable: "Suppose one of you has a hundred sheep and loses one of them. Doesn't he leave the ninety-nine in the open country and go after the lost sheep until he finds it? And when he finds it, he joyfully puts it on his shoulders and goes home. Then he calls his friends and neighbors together and says, 'Rejoice with me; I have found my lost sheep.' I tell you that in the same way there will be more rejoicing in heaven over one sinner who repents than over ninety-nine righteous persons who do not need to repent." Luke 15:1–7 NIV

There are a couple of details in this passage about how we are to treat and accept others that I believe are worthy of highlighting. The first is the manner in which Jesus words the question, "*Doesn't* he leave the ninety-nine in the open country and go after the lost sheep until he finds it?" (Luke 15:4 NIV, italics added)

Think about it: a question in the format of, "Don't you. . ." is asked that way for a couple of possible reasons. One is that we think the answer to that question is obvious; another is that we think we already know the answer to the question and are simply looking for confirmation.

I'm going to guess that for Jesus the answer to that question was obvious. If Jesus's mission for coming to earth was to save us from our sin—or, in other words, save the lost—of *course* he is going to pursue that one lost sheep! He's going after that one lost sheep *every single time*, and that's exactly what he wants us to do. God calls us to be his light in dark places.

How is God using you as a light in dark places, so that those who are lost can be found?

_____

_____

_____

_____

The second detail I want to highlight is that after the lost sheep is found, the man who found that lost sheep _joyfully_ put the sheep on his shoulders as he carried the sheep home. It may seem like a minor detail, but I am a firm believer that Jesus includes details in his stories only if they are necessary to get the point across. Why is it important for us to know that the man joyfully carried the sheep on his shoulders?

Think about your own life. When was the last time you carried something on your shoulders joyfully? What were you carrying?

_____

_____

_____

_____

Has anyone ever joyfully carried something for you? How did it make you feel?

_____

_____

_____

_____

If we treat others and accept them in same way Jesus does, then this is the type of mindset we need to take hold of. We need to pursue the lost until they are found, and we need to do so joyfully—not out of feeling forced to. We are called to do this for *everyone*. Knowing that ninety-nine percent of the sheep were found wasn't good enough for Jesus, and it shouldn't be good enough for us either!

Each of us who is a follower Christ was that one lost sheep before we surrendered our lives to Jesus. We know what it feels like to be lost. That said, how can we be people who claim Christianity and *not* have the mentality of someone who pursues the lost sheep? Talk about selfishness at its finest. I'm not saying maintaining that mentality is easy, and I also don't say that to bring feelings of condemnation. We have all been there and we all have selfishness in our nature, including me.

I made a purposeful decision to leave my story out of my book when I originally started writing because I didn't want the book to be about me—sounds selfless, right? Not really. Writing my story in my book required me to talk about how I lived as the lost sheep—to recall those times in my life that were not very fun, and to articulate those parts well enough to put them on a page.

In order for my book writing to become everything God intended it to be, I had to surrender to him my selfishness of not wanting to include my story in the book. Doing so required me to silence the lies saying, "Your story doesn't matter that much." I also had to surrender my control of who my story reached.

Why didn't I surrender control of who my story reached sooner? Fear. I was afraid what people would think if they knew what I had been through. The problem with that mentality? It's not from God. God uses all parts of our stories for good, and anything telling us otherwise is not God's voice!

What stops you from pursuing the lost in the same way as described in the parable, and how can you surrender that to God?

_____

_____

_____

_____

_____

What is a tangible step you can take toward further being the type of person who leaves the ninety-nine to find the one lost sheep?

_____

_____

_____

_____

_____

—m—

Dear God,

I acknowledge that the obligation I deserve to assume as a result of my sinful nature is death. Thank you for sending your Son to assume the punishment for my sins, and thank you for offering the gift of eternal life as a result of his death. You care for everyone on this earth and accept all who come running toward you. Your care for me is so great that I can cast all my anxiety onto you and know it's in good hands. Reveal the areas of my life that I'm not allowing you to care for so that I can be more intentional in caring for the interests of those around me. Your perfect love bears all things and accepts all parts of my story. You love everyone on this earth enough to leave the ninety-nine to pursue and accept them into your arms, and I ask that you will give me your eyes to see them in the same way.

In Jesus' name,

Amen.

Chapter Twelve

THEY ARE CHOSEN

Lesson 1: Selection

We make choices every day regardless of whether we're aware of it. God gave us the ability to choose from the very beginning of human existence; our ability to choose is called our *free will*. Taking it all the way back to Adam and Eve, the Bible tells us how Eve made a choice to eat of the fruit which led to the first committed sin. But Eve wasn't special—she was just the first person who used her free will to make a choice that led to sin.

Any time we sin, we choose to put our way over God's. At some point, we all choose our way over God's—it's in our human nature. God isn't surprised that we choose our way over his. The good news for us is that we aren't the only ones making choices. Even though we have all chosen our way over God's way, God *still* chooses us and loves us regardless.

"You did not choose me, but I chose you and appointed you that you should go and bear fruit and that your fruit should abide, so that whatever you ask the Father in my name, he may give it to you." John 15:16 ESV

How does it make you feel knowing that God has chosen you even when you haven't chosen him?

_____

_____

_____

_____

<u>**Chosen:**</u> *adjective* selected or marked for special favor or privilege[53]

One of the common ways we make our daily choices is through selection. Our selections can be something as big as buying our next car or as small as what to eat for dinner. In any case, our final selection likely won based on the value we saw it bringing to us over our other potential choices. We are all aware of our tendency to pick the items that bring us the most value. Because of that tendency, when we aren't personally selected for something, our lack of selection can cause us to see ourselves as *less*.

When have you ever viewed yourself as less because you were not selected for something?

_____

_____

_____

_____

---

53 *Merriam-Webster's Dictionary and Thesaurus,* Updated Edition, s.v. "Chosen."

Can you think of a time when someone thought you viewed them as less? How did that effect your relationship?

_____

_____

_____

_____

_____

When we see ourselves as "less" because of not getting selected for something, we allow the world to define our value. God's view of our value remains constant, regardless of whether we are chosen for something. The way God views selection looks a little bit different from the world's view.

The world tries as hard as it can to define our value from as early an age as possible. When God chose me to write books and become a published author, he broke off chains within me that I held onto for almost _twenty years._ The truth is, I kind of liked books when I was little. I even learned how to read before I went to kindergarten, and I read books every night before bed.

Unfortunately, my love for books died quickly because I allowed the world to define my value as early as in first grade. When I started having to read books for grades, I failed to live up to the standards. Week after week, I got reminded of how bad I was at reading books and taking tests. All I could hear or see was, "You suck at reading," and I believed it. The result of my belief? Reading turned into something I hated and I stayed away from books as much as possible.

God selected me to become an author because he didn't let any of the negativity I received as a child change the value he saw in me. In the gospel of Luke, Jesus brings light to this difference and tells a parable to challenge the way view how we make our selections:

When he noticed how the guests picked the places of honor at the table, he told them this parable: "When someone invites you to a wedding feast, do not take the place of honor, for a person more distinguished than you may have been invited. If so, the host who invited both of you will come and say to you, 'Give this person your seat.' Then, humiliated, you will have to take the least important place. But when you are invited, take the lowest place, so that when your host comes, he will say to you, 'Friend, move up to a better place.' Then you will be honored in the presence of all the other guests. For all those who exalt themselves will be humbled, and those who humble themselves will be exalted." Then Jesus said to his host, "When you give a luncheon or dinner, do not invite your friends, your brothers or sisters, your relatives, or your rich neighbors; if you do, they may invite you back and so you will be repaid. But when you give a banquet, invite the poor, the crippled, the lame, the blind, and you will be blessed. Although they cannot repay you, you will be repaid at the resurrection of the righteous." Luke 14:7–14 NIV

Jesus challenges in the way we should go about inviting, or selecting, people. The difference in both mindset and motivation comes into play when looking at where the satisfaction from our selections comes from. Look at the parable. When inviting friends, relatives, and rich neighbors, the satisfaction of our repayment comes from *them*. When inviting the poor, crippled, lame, and blind, the repayment comes from *God*.

If we live our lives driven by how we expect to get repaid by something, we are not living God's will. Jesus took the lowest place for all of us by being humiliated and nailed to the cross for our sin, and he did so purposefully. On the third day, he was taken from that lowest place by rising from the dead and sitting at the right hand of God.

Writing became the first area in my life where I truly committed to something because I felt God calling me to do it and not because I expected to be repaid by it. By uniting to his will and no longer responding to the world's criticism, God took me from an area in which I saw myself as the "lowest" and moved me to a better place.

After two years of many late nights, prayers, tears, and countless cups of coffee, my first book, *Broken Lenses: Identifying Your Truth in a World of Lies*, was chosen for publication. For some, becoming a published author would be fulfilling a life-long dream. For me, it meant inviting God into an area of my brokenness and allowing him to bring restoration. My name will forever be placed on something that once brought me so much hatred—books.

What does taking the lowest place in a situation look like to you?

_____

_____

_____

_____

_____

Have you ever purposefully taken the lowest place in a situation? If so, what was it?

_____

_____

_____

_____

_____

Have you ever invited someone to join you in something knowing that they couldn't repay you? How were you blessed as a result of that situation?

_____

_____

_____

_____

_____

—⁓—

Lesson 2: Marked

If you visit a large farm, you would likely see a flock of livestock marked with a brand roaming the fields. Those who own livestock brand animals as a mark of their ownership, and all animals with the same owner get marked with the same brand. When we leave a mark on something, we make a declaration. By placing the brand on the animals, livestock owners declare which animals belong to them.

In a similar way, God marks out and declares a path for each of us. When we live a life of following God, we follow the path marked out for us by God.

> *Therefore, since we are surrounded by such a great cloud of witnesses, let us throw off everything that hinders and the sin that so easily entangles. And let us run with perseverance the race marked out for us, fixing our eyes on Jesus, the pioneer and perfecter of faith. For the joy set before him he endured the cross, scorning its shame, and sat down at the right hand of the throne of God. Hebrews 12:1–2 NIV*

What is the path that has been marked for you?

_____

_____

_____

_____

_____

How is God using you in the paths he has marked out for others?

_____

_____

_____

_____

_____

A few months after committing to publish my book, I got to hold a physical copy of my book in my hands for the first time. Holding my book was physical representation of the path my life took leading up to that point. That path involved disentangling from the sin of finding fulfillment in alcohol rather than in God, throwing off the worthlessness and emptiness that came from being sexually assaulted, and persevering through thousands of hours of writing in my race to become an author.

Nobody's path is the same. God, the designer of our path, is the only one qualified to judge how those around us are doing in their walk! All we need to do is to recognize that they have a path. Their path won't be the same as ours, but it is just as important as ours. We need to show love to everyone on our path, _regardless_ of where they are on theirs.

There is only one Lawgiver and Judge, the one who is able to save and destroy. But you—who are you to judge your neighbor? James 4:12 NIV "A new commandment I give to you, that you love one another: just as I have loved you, you also are to love one another." John 13:34 ESV

The verse in James directly tells us there's only one Judge qualified to save and destroy, and it's not us. Our lack of qualification means is that God is the only one who has authority to judge how others are doing on their walks.

I can't say I have ever had a monumental turning point kind of experience in life convicting me to judge others less. What I can say is that the more I focused on pursuing the path God marked out for me, the less I cared to engage in activities involving the judgment of others. For me, taking a step to judge others less looks like getting to know their story more. I'm pretty sure this might seem crazy to some, but talking to people I've never met before is one of my favorite activities. Everyone has a unique story and reasons for why they are the way they are. We are called to love them, *not* judge them!

In what ways do you find yourself showing judgment to others on paths that different from yours?

_____

_____

_____

What is a step you can take toward judging the people around you less and loving them more?

_____

_____

_____

_____

_____

To help us walk the path he marked out for us, God marks us with the Holy Spirit when we place our faith in him.

And you also were included in Christ when you heard the message of truth, the gospel of your salvation. When you believed, you were marked in him with a seal, the promised Holy Spirit, who is a deposit guaranteeing our inheritance until the redemption of those who are God's possession—to the praise of his glory. Ephesians 1:13–14 NIV

Note how the above verse states that being marked with the Holy Spirit *guarantees* our inheritance. In other words, God makes a declaration here by saying that all who receive and are marked with the Holy Spirit will receive an inheritance. What does that inheritance look like?

Blessed be the God and Father of our Lord Jesus Christ! According to his great mercy, he has caused us to be born again to a living hope through the resurrection of Jesus Christ from the dead, to an inheritance that is imperishable, undefiled, and unfading, kept in heaven for you, who by God's power are being guarded through faith for a salvation ready to be revealed in the last time. 1 Peter 1:3–5 ESV

God had no obligation to share his inheritance with us. The only reason we have a way to access God's inheritance is because God *chose* to give us access. Everything on earth belongs to him and he gets to decide what happens to all of it. As if the fact that the inheritance is guaranteed wasn't already good enough, what the inheritance consists of makes it even better. Our inheritance from God is imperishable, undefiled, and unfading.

Nothing on this earth can do anything to take it away from us, as it is being stored in heaven for us upon our arrival.

How does knowing that God gives you access to an inheritance you don't deserve change your mindset when it comes to giving to others?

_____

_____

_____

_____

_____

—〰—

Lesson 3: Favor

We've now discussed that for someone to be chosen, they are either selected or marked in some way. However, simply knowing we've been selected or marked for something only begins to scratch the surface when understanding the true beauty behind being chosen. God isn't someone who "selects" something "just because." The reason we are all here right now *isn't* random. Why are we chosen, though? What are we chosen for?

The first reason we are chosen is because of "favor." Nobody asks for a favor unless they *need* something. The reason we need favor can come from a variety of mental, physical, or spiritual needs. If we need something heavy moved, we ask someone for a favor to help us move it. If we have a long to-do list and not enough time to fulfill the items on our list, we ask someone for a favor to help us complete it. When people ask us for a favor, they do so because they think we have the resources to help them.

I am not known for being tall. Occasionally, I need help to reach things up high. In those situations where I need help reaching something up high, from whom do I choose to ask a favor? Am I going to ask a favor from someone shorter than me to reach the item? No, of course not—I'm going to ask someone taller than me. Does that mean I have something against people shorter than me in that moment? No. It simply means that the taller person possessed the *resource* I needed in that moment to help me accomplish my task, and the shorter person didn't.

When was the last time you did a favor for someone? What did you do for them?

_____

_____

_____

_____

_____

When was the last time someone else did a favor for you? What did they do for you?

_____

_____

_____

_____

_____

Showing favor is not below God's pay grade. God knows we all have needs, and he does not hold back in showing us favor. As seen in the following verses, God shows us favor as a product of:

Righteousness: *Surely, LORD, you bless the righteous; you surround them with your favor as with a shield. Psalms 5:12 NIV*

Humility: *Toward the scorners he is scornful, but to the humble he gives favor. Proverbs 3:34 ESV*

Seeking Good: *Whoever seeks good finds favor, but evil comes to one who searches for it. Proverbs 11:27 NIV*

Have you ever been a witness to God's favor? What was the situation that resulted in that favor?

_____

_____

_____

_____

_____

Looking at favor from a human context, we often show favor only to distinct or certain groups of people—we pick favorites. God, however, does not operate in that same context. The qualities of righteousness, humility, and seeking good are qualities every one of us can pursue. Everyone has access to receiving God's favor, and when God says things like he will give favor to the humble, he means it.

One of the biggest ways I knew God chose me to become an author was from all the favor I received in the process. When I began writing, I did so strictly to lead a small group of *maybe* ten people at my home. If it was up to just me, it would've stayed that way. From seeking good and looking to move forward in my passion to lead a women's group, God showed me favor beyond my wildest dream.

My writing went from something I thought was going to reach only people in that small group in my home, to reaching people across the entire country. In the months after I first I held my book I began to prepare for its official launch. I soon found myself on a three-month-long book tour, doing events in eight different states, and getting to share my heart behind the message God chose for me to write to a lot more than ten people. The same kind of favor God has shown to me is available for everyone. God does *not* pick favorites.

> *For God does not show favoritism. Romans 2:11 NIV*

In addition to God's lack of showing favoritism, we are called to be people who do not show favoritism as well.

> *I charge you, in the sight of God and Christ Jesus and the elect angels, to keep these instructions without partiality, and to do nothing out of favoritism. 1 Timothy 5:21 NIV*

How do we become people who do nothing out of favoritism? To be someone who does nothing out of favoritism, we have to be mindful of the way we see value in those around us. We often make our decision to show favor based on the value we see other people bringing to us. The more value they bring us, the more willing we become to bring favor to them. By showing favoritism to people, we create division rather than unity.

We aren't good at hiding our favoritism—people can see right through us when we do certain actions for some people and not for others. If people were to find out they weren't our favorite, how would that make them feel? They would likely start associating with us differently or just completely stop associating with us altogether. None of us on our own strength will ever stop showing favoritism completely though. We need God's favor—and luckily for us, he's willing to give it to us all.

Can you think of a situation where you did not receive something because you were not the favorite in the situation? What were your feelings as a result?

_____

_____

_____

_____

_____

How do you show favoritism?

_____

_____

_____

_____

How could you take a step in the direction of showing less favoritism in some area of your life?

_____

_____

_____

_____

_____

—〰—

Lesson 4: Privilege

The subject of having privilege is one I would argue that our society talks about today more than ever before—we can thank our highly connected and technologically based world for that. In fact, society today wants us to be so aware of what privilege is and the privileges that we have, the phrase "check your privilege" was born. But what is privilege and why is it important enough that the world wants us to make sure we are aware of our personal privileges?

> **Privilege:** *noun* a right or immunity granted as an advantage or favor esp. to some and not others[54]

Part of what it means to be chosen is to be selected for a certain privilege.[55] Viewing privilege in the context of the world looks like certain people or groups having privileges—or special rights—over others. In some cases, people didn't do anything to earn the privilege—it's just a condition of the environment in which they were placed. The unearned privilege of certain people or groups in our world is one I think we are all well aware of. Instead of going deeper into how the world sees privilege, I want to shift the focus of this lesson to what the Bible considers to be a privilege. Some of those privileges include:

> **Serving Christ:** *For you have been given the privilege of serving Christ, not only by believing in him, but also by suffering for him. Philippians 1:29*
>
> **Helping God's People:** *I can assure you that they gave as much as they could, and even more than they could. Of their own free will they begged us and pleaded for the privilege of having a part in helping God's people in Judea. 2 Corinthians 8:3–4*

---

54 *Merriam-Webster's Dictionary and Thesaurus,* Updated Edition, s.v. "Privilege."
55 *Merriam-Webster's Dictionary and Thesaurus,* Updated Edition, s.v. "Chosen."

<u>Sharing the Gospel:</u> *If I did my work as a matter of free choice, then I could expect to be paid; but I do it as a matter of duty, because God has entrusted me with this task. What pay do I get, then? It is the privilege of preaching the Good News without charging for it, without claiming my rights in my work for the gospel. 1 Corinthians 9:17–18*

Have you ever experienced privilege from serving Christ, helping God's people, or sharing the Good News? If so, how?

_____

_____

_____

_____

_____

How have you benefitted from or been privileged by service, help, or sharing of the Good News from others?

_____

_____

_____

_____

_____

Note that these privileges are all mentioned in an outward-facing context. Serving Christ, helping God's people, and sharing the Good News are all focused on how we see and interact with the people around us. Being people who value serving Christ and sharing the gospel won't always be easy and may involve some suffering, but the immunity that comes as a result of these privileges is second to none.

What immunity, or special rights, do these privileges give us?

With one sacrifice, then, he has made perfect forever those who are purified from sin. And the Holy Spirit also gives us his witness. First he says, "This is the covenant that I will make with them in the days to come, says the Lord: I will put my laws in their hearts and write them on their minds." And then he says, "I will not remember their sins and evil deeds any longer." So when these have been forgiven, an offering to take away sins is no longer needed. Hebrews 10:14–18

The immunity and privilege gained from accepting Jesus's sacrifice for our sins is one that nothing or no one else can duplicate. The acceptance of Jesus's offering to pay the price for our sins makes us immune from having to make the payment ourselves—talk about quite the privilege!

Being chosen by God to pursue this road of authorship has been one of the best things that has ever happened to me, but I'd be lying to you if I said it didn't include some suffering along the way. I lived life for twenty-five years following the "American dream." I got the education, landed the good job, and then left it all to pursue a completely different path—a path I didn't know I was capable of walking.

When I tell people I'm an author, their first guess is that I studied some form of English or literature in college. When I tell them that my degrees are in chemistry and business, I almost always get a reaction of, "Wow, that's quite the switch!" They're not wrong, but I wouldn't have my path any other way. Why? Because I know I've been chosen. I get to serve Christ, help God's people, *and* share the gospel through my writing, and it draws me closer to God, too.

Just as I have been chosen, *you* have also been chosen! God brought you on this earth for a reason. He sees you, he respects you, and he loves you dearly.

My prayer for you—for all of us—is to have the eyes to see those around us as God sees. To be people who accept those around us and make it known they are welcome. To be a friend when people are in need, and to see them as the beautiful images of God they are. I pray that through this lifestyle, our communities would be ones that experience the kind of unity God desires, and not the division the enemy thrives on.

Jesus saw every person as valuable enough to die for. Nothing will ever change God's view of our value. I pray that together, *we* can be the people who change this world because we see and interact with other people based on *God's* determination of their value instead of the world's determination of their value.

Have you ever felt like putting in the work to serve Christ wasn't worth the immunity received as a result? Why or why not?

_____

_____

_____

_____

How does knowing you don't have to pay that price allow you to live differently?

_____

_____

_____

_____

Dear God,

Thank you for always choosing to love me. I confess that I don't always make the choice to love you back, but I am grateful that you are there waiting to forgive me when I turn to you. Help me to see those who are on the path that you have marked for me, and give me the power to see those on my path as you see them. Thank you for being a God who does not show favoritism. You are a God who gives favor to all who seek goodness, humility, and righteousness. Renew my mindset on what it means to be chosen by you so that I may see things such as serving you, helping your people, and sharing your good news as privileges rather than burdens.

In Jesus' name,

Amen.

CALL TO ACTION

For more from Emily, check out

and visit www.emilybernathauthor.com

ABOUT THE AUTHOR

Emily began writing out of her passion for women's ministry and wanting to be a light to survivors of sexual assault. As a rape survivor herself, she hit rock bottom, thinking her body had been tainted and that her worth had been taken from her. During this time, she made friends with a group of women who pointed her to God's light and love for her. In being open about her life as a rape survivor, it became apparent to her how many other people experience similar feelings of shame and disgust and allow things that aren't true about them to define them. Through rediscovering her faith and identity in Christ, Emily has found freedom from the shame and condemnation in this world, and she hopes to be able to help others find that same freedom for themselves.

When she's not writing, she speaks and advocates for sexual assault survivors, and serves on the board of Reveal to Heal International; a nonprofit who seeks to shine a light on the Biblical truths of God's love for the broken, oppressed, and victimized. Before beginning her career as an author, she earned a bachelor's degree in chemistry and a master's degree in business administration. She currently resides in Salt Lake City, attends K2 the Church, and spends her free time tutoring, volunteering with her church's youth group, playing soccer, and making latte art.